SOIL SURVEYS AND LAND USE PLANNING

SOIL SURVEYS AND LAND USE
PLANNING

Edited by

L. J. Bartelli
A. A. Klingebiel
J. V. Baird
and
M. R. Heddleson

Published by the
Soil Science Society of America
and
American Society of Agronomy

1966

iv

PROGRAM AND EDITORIAL COMMITTEE

LINDO J. BARTELLI, Chairman
Principal Soil Correlator, Southern States
Soil Conservation Service, USDA
Fort Worth, Texas

J. V. BAIRD
Associate Professor, Fertility Management
North Carolina State University
Raleigh, N. C.

M. R. HEDDLESON
Assistant Professor, Field Crops
Pennsylvania State University
University Park, Pa.

A. A. KLINGEBIEL
Director, Soil Survey Interpretations
Soil Conservation Service, USDA
Washington, D. C.

DENNIS O'HARROW
Executive Director
American Society of Planning Officials
Chicago, Ill.

These papers were presented at the Annual Meetings of the Soil Science Society of America and the American Society of Agronomy at Columbus, Ohio, November 1-5, 1965.

FOREWORD

"Land-use planning" is an expression that we shall be hearing more often in the future. As the population expands, all uses of land and soil become more competitive. Good agricultural land will be under increasing pressure from urban growth and expanding public facilities such as highways and airports. These demands are unique to our time, reflecting the increasing importance of land as living space. It has been estimated that by 1980, over 38 million acres of farm land will be taken over for nonagricultural use. Much of this will be taken from our supply of irreplaceable, highly productive soils because the steep, rough areas are much less desirable for urban and public facility development. Most of the decisions will be irreversible, so the importance of sound land-use planning is evident.

Furthermore, with the ever larger areas of soil being devoted to housing, factories, highways, and the like, there is an increasing danger of costly mistakes in locating structures on soils ill-suited to the particular purpose. In many communities over the country such experience has focused attention on the importance of matching soil characteristics to the requirements for specific uses. Regional and community planners as well as soil scientists are aware of this need. They are joining forces with increasing frequency to deal with problems ranging in scope from broad, regional, land-use planning to specifications for individual structure sites.

The papers published in this book are the result of one of these efforts. They were presented on a special program at the 1965 annual meetings of the Soil Science Society of America and the American Society of Agronomy and were co-sponsored by the American Society of Planning Officials. It is our hope that the experience brought together here will be helpful to those engaged in regional and community planning for the best possible use and conservation of our land resources.

R. W. Pearson, President
Soil Science Society of America

L. A. Richards, President
American Society of Agronomy

vii

PREFACE

Since the end of World War II, the art of planning for urban development has evolved so rapidly that it might be termed a "revolution." The change has come through the introduction of scientific method and knowledge into planning. Now we like to speak of "the art and science of planning," instead of simply "the art of planning." It is doubtful that city planning can ever become completely scientific, but it is already a much better art because of the leavening of science.

In the United States we have had an embarrassment of riches. As we thought of our country before the war, it was an unlimited reservoir of the three basic environmental resources: air, water, and land. We could use these resources in whatever manner desired; there was no end to them in sight.

Not until after World War II did we realize that maybe these resources were not as inexhaustible as previously thought. In fact, the end of the "unlimited" water supply, in the proper place, seemed alarmingly close. We found that there was a limit to the supply of air that could be used both as a sewer and for breathing. There was a limit to the supply in the proper place, such as in the metropolitan center.

Finally, we have discovered that there is even a limit to our supply of land, suitable land of the right kind for urban development, in the proper places. It has been difficult, more so than with water and air, to convince people that all land is not the same, that land has physical characteristics which often are more important than geographic location in planning urban development. Since land is a market commodity, the introduction of the principle that land is a public resource requiring public management based on scientific knowledge has been particularly difficult. And this battle is far from won.

I do believe, however, that the rapidly growing use of soil science—the most recent of the physical sciences to lend a hand to city planning—marks a major step in our progress toward producing better urban environment in our nation. If there were no soil science, I shudder to think of the hodgepodge which would result in trying to care for the 100 million new residents to be added to our urban areas by the end of this century.

The American Society of Planning Officials has been pleased to co-sponsor this meeting with the American Society of Agronomy and the Soil Science Society of America and other conferences on the use of soil science in planning urban development. Soil science is still a new tool for most planners, but I believe that the soil capability analysis soon will be as basic to our art, and science, as the land use inventory, the traffic count, and the population projection.

Dennis O'Harrow, Executive Director
American Society of Planning Officials

CONTENTS

CHAPTER 1

SOIL SURVEYS FOR COMMUNITY PLANNING

Charles E. Kellogg[1]

THE AMERICAN PEOPLE have nearly a hundred thousand kinds of soil, each with a unique combination of characteristics and potentials for use. People in this country have no need to use soils for farming, commercial forestry, housing, recreation, or other purposes unless the soils are suited for that use or can be made so economically.

The great numbers of individual failures among settlers during the push westward in the 19th century stimulated early attempts to study soils in order to find out about the various kinds and how they respond to management. In farming and forestry people learned how to use soil surveys, both for soil selection and for finding out how the kinds of soil on a specific tract of land might respond to management for crops, grasses, and trees. → The same principles of soil use and management that lie back of the great revolution in farm efficiency can be applied as well to the rural space being filled by nonfarm people so rapidly today. The basic soil classification and principles of soil behavior are the same although their interpretations for such use are obviously different. People in this country have no need whatever to put their houses where they will slide down hill, settle and crack, or be flooded; nor where their gardens will be contaminated with sewage effluent; nor where their homes cannot be beautified with growing plants. It has been demonstrated that what has been learned about soil selection for the many specialties in farming can be used for these other purposes.

The principles of managing soils and of controlling water can also be used. A great deal of knowledge gained from research and experience about runoff control, drainage, irrigation, and water storage applies as well to newly developing urban areas as to other land.

So does our knowledge about growing plants. This field has been badly neglected. There is no need for builders to destroy

---

1. Deputy Administrator for Soil Survey, Soil Conservation Service, USDA.

existing trees that add so much to a home and garden. The needless and careless removal of trees and other plants in new developments stimulates some of the worst erosion and siltation to be found. Perhaps even worse is the loss of mature trees for the home site. The new owners then ask for "good," fast-growing shade trees. These are rare in formerly wooded sections to replace the good oaks and hickories unnecessarily torn out by bulldozers. Well-tested and inexpensive methods for saving growing trees and for avoiding soil contamination have long been available.

People now have a new opportunity to develop living space with the advantages of both the country and the city without the slums of either. Within this space they can have fields, forests, parks, water surface, wildlife, and housing. The density of homes can be enough to support efficient schools, shopping areas, and other centers of city life.

The great need for recreational areas is not met by distant parks, but only by local neighborhood areas that young people can walk to from their homes. In most places, if housing were put only where it can be stable and safe, playgrounds and nature-study areas could be easily available where they are most critically needed.

Such housing areas are not limited to the so-called urban fringe around big metropolitan centers. Already in states like New York, farm families have, on the average, six nonfarm neighbors. Clusters of new housing spring up quickly along modern highways both inside and outside incorporated towns and villages.

Your symposium will go into many of these relationships in detail. Mainly, I should like to outline the principles back of soil surveys and their application to community planning.

First of all, the soil survey contributes to our knowledge about soils and gives us the basis for applying to specific tracts of land what has been learned about them through research and experience. The soil map serves as the great bridge for transferring knowledge gained from experience to like soils elsewhere. Since the early thirties, soil scientists have given increasing emphasis to precision in their work and to quantitative interpretations of the behavior of kinds of soil defined within a system of classification. These amount to predictions of what and how much can be expected if a soil is used or manipulated in a specific way.

Useful knowledge for making such predictions about a kind of soil comes in two ways: Through our understanding of its properties and how it functions and through analyses of actual experience in using it. Such empirical results can be depended on even though clear reasons are lacking why a crop management system or a house site succeeded or failed. Accurate soil identification is needed for either process to be helpful.

The more we can base our reasoning on clear principles of soil behavior, the more dependable the results. A combination of evidence is best, so that the predictions arrived at by reasoning from basic principles is consistent with those arrived at from analyses of empirical evidence. Basically, soil classification permits us to classify our knowledge and to remember it and to see relations among soils and between soils and other phenomena. Thus making interpretations or predictions of soil behavior for people to use helps test the soil classification. Soil scientists who make soil surveys for people to use live in "glass houses." Where their maps and interpretations are not accurate, they should and do hear about it.

"A soil" as we use the term in soil science and classification is an individual body on the surface of the earth. It has depth and shape. Its boundaries are also the boundaries of other soils (or of not-soil bodies on the surface of the earth). These boundaries come at places where one or more of the basic soil-forming factors change or have been unlike at some previous time during the genesis of the soil. These factors are: (1) Climate and (2) living matter that act on (3) parent material for soil, as conditioned by (4) relief over periods of (5) time.

Any one of the millions of individual soils has a complex combination of many properties. A soil is a meeting place of the not-soil beneath and the influences of the changing atmosphere and biosphere above. Plants grow in soil. Their roots push the soil particles around. They extract nutrients and water. Microorganisms and animals live and burrow in it. The soil takes in and holds moisture from the atmosphere. Most of the organic wastes of nature are decomposed on it or within it. All its many properties and functions interact with one another. Soil changes during the seasons and even between day and night. If the living matter—the plants, micro-organisms, and animals—change, so does the soil. With geological changes that affect the erosion cycle, the soil changes.

Actually, the soil is so intimately associated with its environment that one cannot take it into a laboratory any more than he can a glacier, a river, or a volcano. All we can take into the laboratory are samples of its parts. To interpret the results of physical, chemical, and biological studies of soil samples one must return to the soil outdoors and integrate the results with all the other unsampled properties and processes.

When man uses the soil he commonly changes it drastically. He plows it, drains it, irrigates it, and fertilizes it for crops. He builds houses and pavements on it. He builds filter fields for sewage within it to take advantage of its great ability to adsorb liquid and to decompose organic matter. So basically, our interest in any soil is not primarily how it is now or how it will function in the natural landscape, but how it will respond to treatment and manipulation.

Individual soils with similar narrow ranges in many properties that combine to give them distinguishing character are placed together as classes in soil classification. Each kind is given a specific name. As our knowledge grows about soils, more and more information is carried by these names. Thus, once we know the name of a soil in any tract of land, all our knowledge about it becomes available for the gardener, the farmer, the rancher, the forester, the engineer, the architect, and the urban planner. The particular information needed by people varies widely, but each goes back to the same basic principles. A person growing alfalfa for example, wants water to enter the soil and be held in available form for use by plants. If he builds a pavement, he wants to keep water out. But the basic principles of soil-water relationships are the same. Thus our first job in using our knowledge about the soils for any tract is to find out their names.

This is not the place to discuss the details of scientific soil classification, but I should like to draw your attention to a few points, which if misunderstood, can lead to great confusion. A kind of soil, as we are using the term here, is a taxonomic class or "taxon;" it includes all the individual soils that fall within its definition.

In making a soil map for people to use, one is limited to a reasonable scale. No one could use a map at a scale of 1:1 on which every soil boundary could be plotted exactly. In the early soil surveys the common scales were about 1 inch to the mile, usually 1:62,500. As the soil surveys began to have more prediction value, people wanted more detail and soil maps were published at 2 inches to the mile. Now the publication scale of most soil maps used in operational planning is 1:20,000 or 1:15,840 (4 inches to the mile). This is about the practical limit for publication. Yet, manuscript soil maps for operational planning may be on even larger scales, up to 1 inch per 100 feet. With none of these scales can the boundaries of each individual soil be traced exactly. The larger the scale the more nearly can we approach exactness. Yet, very large scale maps are nearly valueless for general planning where one wants or needs a view of the soils of a township or a county on one map sheet.

Thus we must continually recall that the soil areas shown on a map and given a specific name can seldom be 100% pure taxonomic units. Each such mapping unit is likely to have some small inclusions of other kinds of soil. That is, as we read a soil map and see areas symbolized as Miami silt loam, it does not mean that every square foot is actually Miami silt loam.

We must also recognize clearly two quite different kinds and functions of soil maps in planning. (1) Communities need a general soil map for use in general planning to show roughly areas for various alternative uses, planned transport, community facilities, and so on. (2) Then they need a detailed soil map for operational planning of specific locations for houses, roads, waterways, parks, and the like. Even these distinctions depend a good deal on the nature of the operations. A soil map satisfactory for operational planning of forests, ranches, and most farms would be considered a general map for planning a highway design, where a working soil map at a scale of 25 or 50 inches per mile may be necessary.

The Soil Survey began seriously in the United States about 1899. During its first 25 years its purpose was mainly to supply maps for soil selection and for estimating systems for using rural land for growing plants--crops, grasses, and trees. It was also during this era that we learned about the soils of the United States and developed reasonably satisfactory methods for their study.

We all know science has been increasing at an exponential rate. Probably we have learned more than twice as much during each 10-year period than we did in the previous one. Furthermore, other sciences came to the aid of soil science. During the late twenties, air photos became available as a base for plotting boundaries between mapping units. This was a great boon to accuracy. We learned a great deal about clay minerals and soil chemistry. But new technology can also create problems for the soil scientist. People now have more powerful machines to move soils around and to shape their surfaces for good or for ill.

Soils engineering first became prominent in the middle period of the Soil Survey, during the late twenties. Empirical tests were developed for measuring selected properties of samples of soil. Some people in the Bureau of Public Roads and elsewhere began to relate these tests and their experience with pavement design to kinds of soil as defined in the system of soil classification.

A prominent and sustained study along this line began in the Michigan State Highway Department in the winter of 1925-26. It

started as a research effort. By soil study and mapping on a
large scale, where paved roads had already been built for some
time, it was hoped that information could be gathered to suggest
what kinds of designs were best for different kinds of soil. These
goals were attained. The more engineers and soil scientists
learned about why pavements failed or did not fail on different
kinds of soil, the more reliable the predictions became. This
procedure became standard for Michigan by 1930 or so.

A great impetus for this integration of soil mechanics and
soil science came with the Second World War. In many military
operations, commanders had to know the engineering properties
of soil in an enemy-held country where they had no possibility of
making tests. It was found that a good soil map for an area
could be estimated by exacting study of the available knowledge
on geology, climate, relief, vegetation, and age of landform. As
we have learned, these five factors combine to make a soil of a
certain kind. With the same combination of these factors, the
soils are identical, or perhaps we should say similar since it is
difficult to measure these factors precisely, to say nothing of
their interactions. Once the estimated soil maps were available
for an area, the engineering interpretations needed in military
operations were made. Commanders can know where tanks are
able to go, where airfields can be built immediately, and all the
rest.

Both old and new soil surveys were interpreted and used in
planning airfields and similar structures in areas under the control of the United States. It obviously occurred to some people
that such kinds of planning had comparable value in planning
houses, roads, and other structures, especially in the expanding
fringes of suburban areas. A few imaginative people were already doing so before some of us in the Soil Survey were aware
of it.

One of the earliest soil surveys made specifically for this
purpose was in Fairfax County, Virginia. A planning group had
been engaged to help county officials make a plan in the early
1950's. They asked for a soil map, which the county did not
have. Arrangements were made with the Virginia State Agricultural Experiment Station and the U. S. Department of Agriculture
to make a soil survey. County officials soon found many uses
for this detailed soil map in both general and operational planning.

Now USDA and the State agricultural experiment stations have
cooperative soil surveys going on in about 75 areas where such
uses are of major importance, to say nothing of the uses being
made of soil maps already printed and available to the public.

Other Federal, State, and local agencies also cooperate in many current soil survey projects.

The planning of communities requires more than the alternative possibilities for use of different kinds of soil and other resources.   It requires the best estimates of future population, industrial development, recreational requirements, educational needs, job opportunities, and other factors that current data make possible.   The goals of local planning boards should not be simply the negative one of avoiding trouble but the positive one of economic development and efficient services to meet the needs of the people, at least for a generation.

CHAPTER 2

SOIL SURVEYS AND THE REGIONAL LAND USE PLAN

Robert H. Doyle[1]

CONSTRUCTION, research, and testing activities at the Cape Kennedy space center (then called Cape Canaveral) during the decade prior to 1962 had generated an economic transformation unprecedented in the peacetime history of the United States. Explosive growth conditions in and around the Cape created problems and potentials that demanded long-range as well as immediate attention. A multi-county organization was needed to assemble information and provide guidance to cope with the chaotic situation. In February 1962, appointed representatives from the six Florida counties nearest the Cape met to establish a Regional Planning Council.

The Council assigned top priority to early completion of a region-wide plan for future development. Such a task was indeed formidable. The six-county area covered more than 6,000 square miles, contained almost 700,000 people, and had experienced little or no comprehensive planning at any level of government.

After recruiting a small, professionally-trained planning staff, the Council embarked in late 1962 upon what turned out to be a unique work program. This program produced the desired plan in the remarkably short time of less than 12 months. Financed in part by a grant from the federal Housing and Home Finance Agency, key activities included:

1) Retention of a qualified consultant to furnish aerial photographs and appropriate base maps of the entire Region. Through interpretation of the new photographs, an up-to-date inventory of existing land use patterns was quickly accomplished.

2) Formation of two special advisory groups. The first of these, designated as "Panel A," was composed of state agency officials, university representatives, and a soil scientist from the USDA Soil Conservation Service in Gainesville. The second group, of "Panel B," was made up of nationally recognized specialists in fields such as population forecasting, industrial development, resource conservation, and

---

1. Executive Director, East Central Florida Regional Planning Council.

8

transportation planning. Both panels supplied the Council with useful information and recommendations as to how the plan could best be developed, refined, and implemented.

3) Sponsorship of numerous community workshops held through-out the Region to solicit local advice and participation. Elected and administrative officials in each area took part in these workshops, along with the general public.

4) Accumulation by the Council staff of basic information about the Region's economy, population, land use trends, and natural resources.

5) Preparation of a preliminary plan through a correlation of panel findings, workshop recommendations, and pertinent background materials. This part of the work was also a staff function.

6) Presentation of this "plan of concepts" to the two panels, participating county commissions, and many other interested groups during the summer of 1963. Following these reviews, an illustrated report describing the plan was prepared and published near the end of 1963.

Every possible device to speed the normal pace of plan development was utilized in carrying out the program. Compiling the land-use inventory by means of air photo interpretation rather than by field surveys saved months of time. Firsthand information was channeled directly into the project through the specialist teams and local workshops. Identifying major considerations at an early stage helped avoid time-consuming work on less significant details.

Of all the expedients used, however, perhaps none was more valuable than a special soil survey analysis made for the Council by the Soil Conservation Service, USDA, and the Florida Agricultural Experiment Station. By pointing up troublesome soil conditions in various locales within the Region, this analysis supplied documented justification for many of the land-use recommendations incorporated in the Regional Plan.

PROFILE OF THE SOIL SURVEY ANALYSIS

Presented by means of several large colored maps of the soils of the Region and supported by selected soil interpretations, a soil survey report was made available to the Council in early 1963. As stated in the report, proper utilization of soils information in land-use planning should logically follow a three-step sequence:

First. A general soil map is needed for broad land use planning. It makes possible an over-all "broad stroke" study of available soil resources early in the planning process. Such a preview involves consideration of limitations, restrictions, or hazards for use relative to the various general soil areas involved.

Second. A detailed soil map is needed for a careful study of individual kinds of soil as classified and mapped in accordance with given areas of interest. Detailed soil maps are essential in considering limitations, restrictions, or hazards for use at this stage of planning.

Third. On-site studies of the soil after planning has progressed to the point of determining specific uses for specific areas.

Since the Council was then working on a broad-scale plan, and inasmuch as detailed soil surveys for most of the Region were not available at that time, the soils study was confined solely to the first step of this sequence.

The completed soil survey identified the different kinds of soil and focused the interpretations on 16 significantly different types of geographic soil areas recognizable in East Central Florida. Each of these 16 areas, or "soil-associations," consists of a combination of soils that occur in characteristic and repeating patterns. The combinations analyzed range from excessively drained, undulating sandy soils such as the St. Lucie-Lakewood association, to almost level, very poorly drained peats and mucks like the Brighton-Everglades association. Fresh water swamp areas and tidal marshes were also separated and studied.

Although literally dozens of land uses could have been treated in the study, the soil scientists selected ten that held special significance for the Region. The soils were rated according to their limitations for the following uses:

1. Dwelling houses and light industry
2. Septic tank drainage fields
3. Roads and railroads
4. Airport runways
5. Hunting areas
6. Campgrounds and picnic areas
7. Sports areas (golf courses, etc.)
8. Cultivated crops
9. Range
10. Forest (slash pine)

Because soil requirements for light industry are very similar to those for residences, the two uses were grouped together for

purposes of analysis. Conversely, road and railroad uses were separated from airport runaways because of differences in engineering
requirements.

Eleven important characteristics or qualities, listed as follows,
were evaluated in determining the ability of soil combinations in
various geographic areas to accommodate different land uses:

1. Slope
2. Wetness
3. Permeability
4. Depth of rock
5. Susceptibility to erosion
6. Shrink-swell potential
7. Presumptive bearing value
8. California bearing value
9. Corrosion potential
10. Trafficability
11. Overflow or flooding hazard

Some of these—slope and wetness, for example—have an important bearing on practically all possible uses, both urban and
rural. Others, such as corrosion potential, affect just a few uses
and then only under certain conditions.

With 16 soil associations to deal with, 10 land-use types to test,
and 11 characteristics and qualities to consider, the soil scientists
had to make hundreds of value judgments. To assist in this process,
they employed a 5-class weighted rating system designed to reflect
the severity and type of problems that would be encountered if a
given use is located within a particular soil association. Expressed
in terms of soil limitations, restrictions, or hazards for a particular
use, a rating of 1 indicates none; 2 - slight; 3 - moderate; 4 - severe; and 5 - very severe.

Table 1 is representative of the results obtained by this seem-
ingly complex effort. By applying the rating scale, it can readily be
seen that soils in the St. Lucie-Lakewood soil association are well
suited for septic tank drainage fields. On the other hand, severe soil
problems should be expected if dwelling houses and light industry
locate in these areas. This kind of direct, factual information--
especially when portrayed on maps in appropriate colors—is an invaluable planning resource.

USE OF THE SOIL SURVEY FOR PLANNING PURPOSES

The general soil maps and interpretations included in the soil
survey report have proved their value and versatility. In addition to

Table 1. Rating of soil associations according to limitations
of the soil for selected land uses.

Soil associations	Percent of area	Dwelling houses & light industry	Septic tank drainage fields	Roads and railroads	Airport runways	Hunting areas	Camp grounds and picnic areas	Sports areas	Cultivated crops	Range	Forest (slash pine)
St. Lucie-											
Lakewood	50	4	1	3	3	4	4	4	4	5	4
wood	25	3	1	3	3	3	2	3	4	5	4
Pomello	25	3	2	3	3	3	2	3	4	4	3
Summary rating		4	1	3	3	4	3	4	4	5	4
Palm Beach-											
Coastal	80	3	1	3	3	3	2	3	3	5	4
Dunes	10	5	1	-	-	-	-	-	5	5	5
St. Lucie	5	4	1	3	3	4	4	4	4	5	4
Summary rating		3	1	3	3	3	2	3	4	5	4
Lakeland-											
Blanton	45	2	1	3	3	2	1	2	3	4	3
(High)	40	2	1	3	3	2	1	2	3	4	3
Eustis	10	2	1	2	2	2	1	2	3	4	3
Summary rating		2	1	3	3	2	1	2	3	4	3

their major role in shaping the preliminary plan, these interpretations are strongly influencing the detailed plan now being prepared.

Instances of how soil survey information can be of value are not hard to find, and East Central Florida's experience provides many. The following examples serve to illustrate some of the ways in which soil maps and interpretations can be used for regional planning purposes.

1) Predicting urban growth areas. Determining the direction and extent of urban expansion is usually one of the more perplexing problems that face a land-use planner, particularly if the planning area includes a fast-growing inland community unhampered by natural physical barriers such as a mountain range or a wide river. Orlando, the largest city in the six-county Region, is such a community.

When the existing land-use pattern was superimposed on the colored interpretive soil survey maps, it was easy to see that Orlando's past development had largely followed favorable soil conditions. Other communities in the Region showed the same tendency. Gaps in urban development almost invariably turned out to be soils poorly suited for urban use. With this clue, the probable format of future expansion was much easier to predict. In the absence of overriding economic or other special factors, the soil maps serve to flag probable new growth areas.

2) Reserving open areas. Increasing awareness at all levels of government of the obligation to reserve suitable open space for succeeding generations inspired the Council to include in the preliminary plan a vast nonurban preserve designated as the St. Johns Greenway. Generally following the course of the St. Johns River, which runs from south to north through the heart of the Region, The Greenway is intended to serve as a permanent open space buffer between the inland and coastal population concentrations. Once more, the soil maps proved their worth by helping to define the boundaries of this important concept.

3) Identifying water recharge areas. An accurate picture of available water resources was considered to be essential by the Council. By grouping soil associations, as shown on the soil maps, according to various hydrologic characteristics, the staff found that water recharge and discharge areas could be identified at an early stage. A detailed water resource study made for the Council by a geological engineering firm subsequently confirmed the general accuracy of these tentative identifications.

4) Recognizing potential use conflict areas. If areas likely to generate potential use conflicts can be identified prior to development, such conflicts can be at least minimized and may be avoided altogether. The special soil maps and their interpretations were also helpful in this facet of planning. Within the six-county area, the soil association maps clearly identified lands ideal for citrus uses that also happened to be ideal for housing projects. Alerted to this condition, the Council urged that low density development standards be adopted in some parts of the Region in an effort to ward off undesirable urban encroachment on high quality agricultural soils.

5) Refining broad land use categories. In its preliminary plan, the Council used the category "agriculture and idle land" for areas not earmarked for urban, conservation or special needs. Since the refined version of the first plan (now nearing completion) is considerably more detailed, this category has been subclassified into primary and secondary agricultural areas. Again, soil maps served as a prime resource for this operation.

A number of other illustrations could be cited. However, the above examples adequately mirror the benefits received by the Regional Planning Council as a result of having soil survey information available for use.

CONCLUSION

In the past, long-range plans for multi-county or multi-state regions centered on resource conservation. Other factors, if treated at all, received only superficial attention; the heavy emphasis was on preservation of land, water and mineral resources. Some of these efforts were outstandingly successful in achieving their stated objectives. The vast Tennessee Valley Authority is a prime example, as is the Muskingum Water Conservancy District project in Ohio. Dozens of other similar studies, however, have accomplished little or nothing.

Today's inexorable trends are bringing regional planning into ever-greater prominence in the United States. The movement from farm to city and from small town to metropolis is producing problems that extend far beyond the boundaries of local political jurisdictions. Moreover, in recognition of these trends new federal and state programs are increasingly turning to the regional approach.

Natural resource conservation is therefore but one of many considerations in the current regional context. Economic determinants, transportation requirements, industrial development potentials, inter-government arrangements, urban-rural relationships—these are some of the factors that can no longer be ignored. Today's programs are "people oriented" and the key word in planning is "comprehensive."

Groups that have traditionally studied natural resources such as the soil itself have a vital role to play in this changing process. Techniques may have to be expanded and new skills acquired if the resource specialist is to fulfill his mission. But, as the East Central Florida Plan so clearly shows, the soil scientist is badly needed to help fit all of the many pieces of the puzzle together.

CHAPTER 3

SOILS AND THEIR ROLE IN PLAN-NING A SUBURBAN COUNTY

David B. Witwer[1]

"The Northeastern seaboard of the U.S. is today the site of a remarkable development—an almost continuous stretch of urban and suburban areas from southern New Hampshire to northern Virginia and from the Atlantic shore to the Appalachian foothills. . . No other section of the U.S. has such a large concentration of population, with such a high average density, spread over such a large area."
Jean Gottman   Megalopolis

MONTGOMERY COUNTY, Pennsylvania, is a small part of the now almost continuous East coast megalopolis. It occupies 492 square miles and is comprised of 62 municipalities. A part of Philadelphia is in Montgomery County.

Within the confines of the county, there is a blend of urban, suburban, and rural living. Once an important agricultural county, but now recognized as a major industrial and residential center, Montgomery County has experienced rapid population growth. From 1920 to 1960, the population almost tripled, increasing from 200,000 to 517,000 people. At this growth rate, the population will at least double by the year 2000, resulting in over 1,200,000 people. Approximately 80% of the population is within an urban or suburban setting, distributed unevenly throughout the county and occupying about 40% of the total land area.

INITIATION OF SOIL SURVEY

From a one-time setting of small towns centering around industries which straddled the banks of a river front and rural communities situated near the crossroads of travel, the county has evolved into a heterogeneous mixture of land uses. Today, the vast stretches of farms and open spaces that were once so prevalent are being transformed into a society traversed by

1. Chief, Cartographic Section, Montgomery County Planning Commission, Norristown, Pennsylvania.

countless transportation arteries and composed of residential subdivisions, institutions, shopping centers, and industrial parks.
The county is experiencing the effects of a new frontier, not unlike the days of the Gold Rush, which can be described today as
the great Land Rush. This Land Rush, or race for space, has
descended upon the county and its effects will remain for all time.

The Montgomery County Commissioners, the officials of the
County Planning Commission, and the Soil and Water Conservation
District were concerned over this dilemma of vanishing open
space and understood that there was a need to obtain basic soils
information that would contribute to all phases of land use planning. The county officials realized that a modern soil survey
was a vital necessity and made an agreement among county, state
and federal agencies to accelerate the completion of a soil survey.

Through a cost share arrangement a contract was signed by
the County Commissioners, the Pennsylvania Department of Agriculture, and the Soil Conservation Service, U.S. Department of
Agriculture.

The survey to be undertaken was a "Standard Detailed Soil
Survey of Medium Intensity" with special emphasis and detail on
urban planning applications, in addition to the traditional agricultural uses. Work began on an acre-by-acre basis of the county's
492 square miles. Soils were tested to a depth of 2.5 to 8 feet
below the surface and it is estimated that 750,000 auger holes
were made during the survey.

The County Planning Commission, in agreement with the Soil
Conservation Service, established survey priorities in order to
integrate survey findings with ongoing comprehensive planning
studies, and the review and analysis of proposed subdivisions.

APPLICATIONS OF SURVEY FINDINGS

Arrangements were made with the Soil Conservation Service
to use copies of the field sheets prior to final map compilation
and printing of the soil maps and report. An interim report containing soil description and intepretation was also prepared for
immediate use.

Preliminary information was received in the form of 9 = x 9-
inch aerial photograph negatives at a scale of 1" = 1,320', which
were reproduced from the soil scientist's field sheets. These
sheets were complete with all the necessary information indicated
by the standard soil mapping legend including soil type, slope,
erosion, and detailed information such as made-land, quarries,

and other valuable resources locations. Negative diazo prints of the field sheet negatives were produced, since this proved to be a most economic and efficient manner of initial reproduction.

Armed with these negative prints and considerable information about the 240 different kinds of soil, staff planners of the Commission set out to apply the early results in a number of ways. It is interesting to note that this early use of the soil data benefitted the county in that it could focus its attention on areas of prime concern immediately without awaiting the completion of the field survey and the final publication.

Considerable time and effort were placed on the preparation and compilation of interpretative maps, as the aerial photos included the distortions that one normally encounters, in addition to the problems of transcribing data to a suitable base map. There was, also, a problem of scale, as most township base maps are at a scale of 1" = 800', while the soil survey field sheets were at a scale of 1" = 1320'. Where soil surveys have been completed the map sheets contained in the published soil survey can be used or mylar positives of these sheets can be reproduced at any desired scale for use. This will aid greatly in compiling the information.

Several methods of reproduction were investigated, including: (1) Reduction of municipal base maps to the soil mapping scale and then compiling at scale; (2) Enlargement of soil field sheets to municipal map scale by vertical overhead projector equipped with a standard 9 x 9" aerial photograph frame; (3) Enlargement of soil field sheets to municipal map scale by standard photographic reproduction; (4) Micro film (35 mm) and then enlarging back to suitable scale by a reader-printer; (5) Utilization of micromaster process (105 mm) and blowback to desired scale. Step 1 was used involving a reduction of municipal base maps to the soil field sheet scale of 1" = 1320' and then compiling the data. These preliminary investigations and soil interpretations led to the development of two significant maps: (1) Alluvial Soils—Areas Subject to Flooding and Slope, and (2) The Suitability of Soils for the On-Site Disposal of Sewage.

ALLUVIAL SOILS AND STEEPNESS OF SLOPE

Alluvial soils are formed from sediments deposited by flood waters, located on level or near-level areas along streams. The land areas covered by these alluvial soils are subject to periodic inundations of short duration which may occur several times a year to once in several years.

While the development of lands located within this alluvial soil areas is not an engineering impossibility, it is generally unwise due to the extreme cost and design factors that must be considered in overcoming periodic inundation, high water tables, unstable soil conditions, and other problems of varying complexity. It is rare that flood plain lands can be developed advantageously in light of the existing availability of lands and their values in suburban areas. A noteworthy exception is the Fort Washington Industrial Park area. This park lies in the heart of the flood plain and has been engineered by extensive stream rechannelling and land fill operations. Such developments of flood plains are beyond the reach of most smaller scaled operations and their apparent success is subject to future experiences and should be seriously considered before developing areas of this nature. Another more serious problem that confronts one who attempts to develop flood plains by rechannelling and land fill operations is that of upsetting nature's balance in the processes of stream evolution and aquifer recharge, which, in turn, adversely affect vegetation and animal life.

The location of alluvial soils and the steepness of slope as interpreted from the soil survey maps are shown on Figures 1 and 2. The categories in use by planners are: 0-3% (alluvial soils), typified as being flat land; 0-8%, flat to gently sloping; 8-15%, moderately sloping; and over 15%, considered as excessively steep. The areas of flat land and excessively steep slopes are normally planned for as open space uses. The greater majority of land uses are planned for on gentle to moderate slopes, since development problems on these slopes are less difficult to overcome.

SOIL DRAINAGE CHARACTERISTICS

The drainage characteristics of soils are extremely important in areas undergoing development. This is especially true in areas which are not served by public sewer facilities and where on-site sewage disposal systems will have to be used for years to come. It is difficult to justify the premature installation of public sewers in areas where the density of development does not warrant them.

Of equal importance is the avoidance of on-site disposal systems where they cannot be expected to function properly over a period of time. The apparent success of these systems in operation may or may not indicate their future abilities to function adequately as the density of development increases. There is

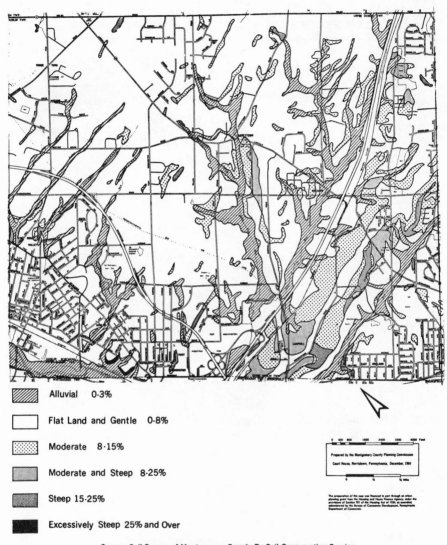

Alluvial   0-3%

Flat Land and Gentle   0-8%

Moderate   8-15%

Moderate and Steep   8-25%

Steep 15-25%

Excessively Steep 25% and Over

Source: Soil Survey of Montgomery County By Soil Conservation Service
of the U.S. Department of Agriculture 1960-63

Figure 1. Map showing location of alluvial soils and steepness of slope in upper Dublin Township.

always the danger of ground water contamination and stream pollution even when the system seems to be functioning properly. While wet basements and cracked foundations may not be the concern of municipal governments, they are frequently the by-product

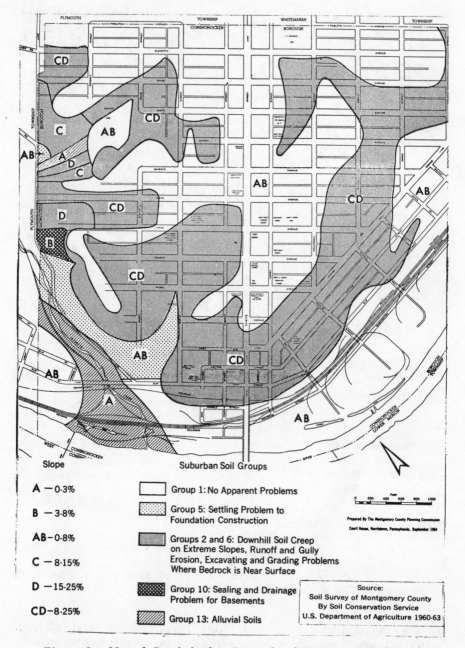

Figure 2.   Map of Conshohocken Borough, showing some soil problems important to urban planning.

of a development constructed on poorly drained soils. It is, therefore, critical that public officials and private citizens work together to control the use and design of on-site systems where they must be used, while simultaneously planning for the orderly development of public sewers and water.

To illustrate these difficulties to various municipalities, the soils were placed into five capability groups showing degrees of soil limitations for on-site sewage disposal as influenced by soil drainage. The soil properties affecting this classification include permeability, porosity, seasonal and permanent high water tables, slope, hillside seepage, soil creep, erosion, surface runoff, hardpan layers, depth of soil to bedrock, and others. The four categories used in Plate 1 (see page 181) are: (1) Satisfactory - soils suitable for on-site disposal sewage; (2) Satisfactory, but with caution - soils generally suitable for on-lot disposal facilities, but ground water contamination is probable due to a high water table close to surface; (3) Variable - soils that may be satisfactory providing the subsoil is permeable. Also included in this category are steep slopes with shallow soils resulting in nearness of bedrock to surface; (4) Unsatisfactory - those soils which are not satisfactory for use because of the presence of impervious water restricting layers, alluvial soils, high water tables, etc. A fifth category termed "Madeland" must also be included as possibly unsatisfactory use due to earth-moving in urban and suburban developments that has removed or altered the characteristics typical of the original soils in the location.

Plate 1 shows considerable areas of the municipality that are unsatisfactory, indicating that the different kinds of soil and slope can play an important role in the orderly development of any community. The rapid advances in modern-day soil survey techniques and methodology are invaluable in planning for the future development of municipalities. Soil capabilities including slope for on-site disposal provide important guide lines for the development of residential areas and also give information in planning for the extensions of public sewer and water facilities. These indicators also play an important part in determining specific sites for commercial, institutional and industrial location. The soil survey also shows areas of excessively steep slopes and areas subject to flooding that can be preserved for open space use.

SOIL SURVEYS AND COUNTY PLANNING

Soil survey data have been applied to all municipalities undergoing comprehensive planning in order to recommend land uses

in accordance with soil conditions. At present over 80% of the
county has or is being planned for and the results of the soil
survey are being utilized throughout. It should be noted that soil
interpretations are only one criteria for recommending land uses.
There are many other factors including the goals of a community,
population, growth, traffic intensities, and economy - to mention
only a few. In some instances it may be desirable to overcome
the limitations of the soil through proper design for a specific
use.

Soils information is presently being used in two comprehensive
planning areas of the county comprising some 150 square miles.
Figure 3 is a generalized map of one of these areas illustrating
Soils Unsuitable for Development, based on high water tables, excessive slope, and flood plains. This is a generalized map and
its sole use is for area planning. As the studies progress, attention will be given to detailed soil maps. Since this area is predominately rural in nature, emphasis will be placed on the traditional use of the soil survey - agricultural capabilities and cropland yields.

INTERIM SOIL SURVEY REPORT

Another major use of the soil survey information has been
the evaluation of each land subdivision proposal submitted to the
Planning Commission for review and/or approval. This is to
enforce that section of the county code which stated that all municipalities must submit land subdivision to the County Planning
Commission for review. The soil survey has been an invaluable
guide to aid the staff subdivision planner in making his recommendations to developers, municipal planning commissions, engineers, and property owners.

The interim soil survey report consists of a general soil
map showing the various soil associations including names of soil,
mapping units, their group numbers, and other pertinent data.
Descriptions of each of the named soils in the survey area and
interpretations important to the use of the soils in the report including such information as (1) Suitability of soil for on-site disposal of sewage; (2) Internal soil drainage (wetness); (3) Surface
run-off; (4) Water table condition; (5) Soil suitability for foundations of roads and small buildings; (6) Depth to bedrock; (7) Other
soil limitations; and (8) Recommendations for development use -
based on soil properties.

UPPER PERKIOMEN VALLEY MONTGOMERY COUNTY, PENNSYLVANIA

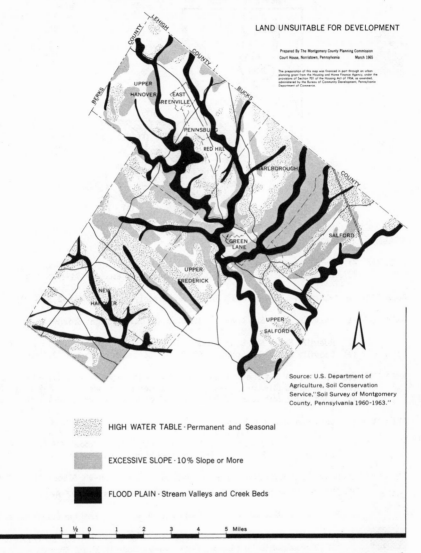

LAND UNSUITABLE FOR DEVELOPMENT

Prepared By The Montgomery County Planning Commission
Court House, Norristown, Pennsylvania   March 1965

The preparation of this map was financed in part through an urban
planning grant from the Housing and Home Finance Agency, under the
provisions of Section 701 of the Housing Act of 1954, as amended,
administered by the Bureau of Community Development, Pennsylvania
Department of Commerce.

Source: U.S. Department of
Agriculture, Soil Conservation
Service,"Soil Survey of Montgomery
County, Pennsylvania 1960-1963."

HIGH WATER TABLE - Permanent and Seasonal

EXCESSIVE SLOPE - 10% Slope or More

FLOOD PLAIN - Stream Valleys and Creek Beds

1 ½ 0   1   2   3   4   5 Miles

Figure 3.   General soil map of upper Perkiomen Valley, showing soils unsuitable for development.

This interim report was instrumental in the proposed development of a "cluster" subdivision.   The soil survey was useful in indicating the soils of the proposed development, as seen in Figure 4 and in Plate 2 (page 182), and the design factors, taking into consideration: problems of alluvial soils, high water tables,

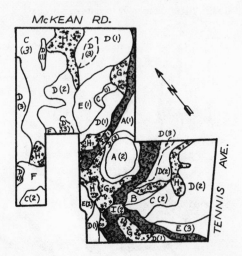

SCALE: 1"= 1320'

AREA "A": (1)   Lansdale Silt Loam, 0-3% Slope, Moderately Eroded (71-A-2,S.G.1)
           (2)   Lansdale Silt Loam, 3-8% Slope, Moderately Eroded (71-B-2,S.G.1)

AREA "B": Penn-Lansdale Loams, 0-3% Slope, Moderately Eroded (72-A-2,S.G.7)

AREA "C": (1)   Reaville Shaly Silt Loam, 0-3% Slope, None to Slight Erosion
                     (315-A-1,S.G.10)
           (2)   Reaville Shaly Silt Loam, 0-3% Slope, Moderately Eroded (315-A-2,S.G.10)
           (3)   Reaville Shaly Silt Loam, 3-8% Slope, Moderately Eroded (315-B-2,S.G.10)

AREA "D": (1)   Readington Silt Loam, 0-3% Slope, None to Slight Erosion (316-A-1,S.G.10)
           (2)   Readington Silt Loam, 0-3% Slope, Moderately Eroded (316-A-2,S.G.10)
           (3)   Readington Silt Loam, 3-8% Slope, Moderately Eroded (316-B-2,S.G.10)

AREA "E": (1)   Lawrenceville Silt Loam, 0-3% Slope, None to Slight Erosion
                     (36-A-1,S.G.10)
           (2)   Lawrenceville Silt Loam, 0-3% Slope, Moderately Eroded (36-A-2,S.G.10)
           (3)   Lawrenceville Silt Loam, 3-8% Slope, Moderately Eroded (36-B-2,S.G.10)

AREA "F": Made Land, Triassic Shale and Sandstone Materials, 0-8% Slope (MT-AB,S.G.10)

          "G": Croton Silt Loam, 0-3% Slope, None to Slight Erosion (103-A-1,S.G.12)

          "H": Abbottstown Silt Loam, 0-3% Slope, None to Slight Erosion (317-A-1,S.G.12)

          "I": (1)   Rowland Silt Loam, 0-3% Slope, None to Slight Erosion (5-A-1,S.G.13)
                (2)   Bowmansville Silt Loam, 0-3% Slope, None to Slight Erosion
                          (6-A-1,S.G.13)

Figure 4. Description of soils in area surveyed, Horsham Township.

and restricting soil layers. Since public sewers were proposed
for the area, many of the unsatisfactory conditions found on site
were not critical design factors. The "cluster" was also included
in the comprehensive plan of the municipality and ultimately led

to an ordinance on cluster development that was adopted in the county.

In general, the cooperation of engineers, surveyors and developers concerning the use of the interim soil survey report has been satisfactory. Many people now come to the commission with sketch plans before the expense of actual plans are undertaken.

The Pennsylvania Department of Health has made extensive use of soils information as an aid for the environmental health survey of each intended development. In Montgomery County, the Health Department has established a required procedure that all developers must follow prior to approval or rejection of proposed sanitary systems in municipalities where they have jurisdiction. The sanitarians within the county were trained in the use of soil surveys and developed a work sheet that must be followed by all developers taking into account the following: (1) public sanitary sewers - the most desirable method of sewage disposal; (2) an interim or permanent small sewage treatment plant - interim plants serving an area during a period until public sewers may be provided; (3) subsurface septic tank systems - public sewers or small treatment plant not being feasible. Consideration is given a septic tank system where soils are favorable based on information from the soil survey. Where soils have little or no absorptive capabilities or when sewage could possibly contaminate ground water, septic tanks are naturally unsatisfactory.

The Health Department requires that the developer submit a Soil Capability Analysis Report for consideration and requires that certain criteria be followed for (1) tile field installation, and (2) sewage pit installation including information on percolation, depth and height of water table, certification by a professional engineer, and design criteria acceptable to the department.

In most cases, the results of the soil survey as compared with measured percolation tests performed under satisfactory field conditions have proven to be very accurate. This reveals the accuracies of field survey techniques made by soil scientists.

Percolation tests are often run in the summer time when the soils are dry and the water table is deep in the soil. Under these conditions the percolation tests appear to be adequate but during wet periods when the water table is high the percolation test would not be satisfactory. A soil map will show those soils that have seasonal water tables or impervious layers where septic tank filter fields are likely to fail. For this reason the percolation test and the soil map may not agree. In such cases the soil map is a more reliable guide to use than the percolation test.

In most instances, there is no legislation to prohibit percolation tests being taken during favorable season (dry periods) of the year and there is some question as to the reliability of the methods and techniques used by individuals in reporting such percolation information even though the Health Department standards are purported to be followed. While it is a known fact that soils mapped as a particular name type are 85% accurate, it is also realized that percolation tests are considerably less accurate when used as the only criteria for testing on-site capabilities. Percolation tests as such, are recognized as being in many cases wholly inadequate, so the soil survey data have been used as the prime factor in determining on-site capabilities for sewage disposal. Local drought conditions such as experienced in Pennsylvania over the past four years have caused many problems in convincing engineers and developers that times are not normal. It is expected that many systems that were put in under these conditions will fail to operate adequately under normal wet seasons.

A study is currently underway to examine the fluctuation of high water tables over a period of several years. Presently, it is necessary that a soil scientist be called upon to investigate on-site areas in question, which have supposedly favorable percolation tests, as indicated by the engineers. This is done to investigate the possible presence of high water tables and other detrimental soil characteristics which could interfere with the satisfactory operation of on-site disposal systems. As these data on high water tables become available and correlated with the soil maps and the percolation tests, more reliable estimates can be made for on-site sewage disposal.

As evidenced by on-site sewage suitability maps prepared from soil maps of municipalities in the county, much of the land area is unsuitable for on-site disposal techniques. It is not reasonable to expect that developments would cease under these conditions, but by utilizing the soil survey and intelligently planning those areas that are suitable for on-site sewage disposal, it is possible to guide the proper development of communities.

One may question the ability of a soil to handle sewage effluent and state that larger lots are the answer; however, larger lots do not make public sewers economically feasible in the future. The on-lot systems in most cases do not really answer the problem of poor soils and their ability to accept or reject effluent. Large lot zoning is really only an attempt to slow development in the majority of cases until the time comes when sewers are available. But it must be pointed out that when large lot development occurs, the economic feasibility of providing public sewers is impractical in many cases due to the front footage cost per dwelling unit and the rather extensive land areas that must be traversed when providing the trunk line. The Health Department, primarily, and the soil scientist should investigate on-site systems which will operate for a duration of 2 to 3 years, particularly in the grey area of moderately well-drained soils. It is in this area that further research should be conducted. There have been systems in many areas in this county that are reported to be working adequately under "certain" conditions to provide on-site use until public sewers become available.

FLOOD PLAIN CONSERVATION DISTRICT ORDINANCE

In 1964, staff planners of the County Planning Commission prepared a model ordinance known as the "Flood Plain Conservation District Ordinance."

For some time it had been realized that the traditional flood plain ordinance was far too elaborate and that techniques necessarily utilized in the preparation of such a document could not be justified on minor streams and tributaries. The cost of detailed flood plain studies for large creeks and streams was far too expensive and elaborate to be applied to smaller tributaries. This model was prepared in a fashion that the survey information could be readily applied in the case of smaller streams.

A flood plain as defined by the model includes: "those areas subject to frequent periodic flooding and delineated as alluvial soils by the Soil Conservation Service, U.S. Department of Agriculture, in the Soil Survey of Montgomery County, 1960-1963. Although infrequent floods will exceed the limits of alluvial soils, these alluvial soils, which are water deposited soils, represent the areas most often inundated by flood waters and represent the most realistic flood plain. . . . These maps and data shall become part of the Municipal Zoning Map."

Permitted and prohibited uses are stated in the model and include a statement that the Planning Commission approve or reject: "all plans for structures within a distance of 100 feet from the Flood Plain Conservation District and all plans for development of a recreational utility use within or adjacent to the District. . ."

A built-in safety factor was incorporated and pertains to exceptions: "Insofar as various natural conditions, including the flood plain as herein defined, may change, such change can be validated by detailed on-site survey techniques approved by the

Soil Conservation Service, U.S. Department of Agriculture. The delineation of the flood plain boundary as shown on the soil maps can be modified by the Zoning Board of Adjustment upon receipt of the findings of the detailed on-site survey techniques by the petitioner. The Zoning Board of Adjustment shall act only upon the affirmative recommendations of the Municipal Planning Commission and the validation of the Soil Conservation Service and/or other appropriate agencies." The Flood Plain Conservation District Ordinance therefore becomes a part of the municipal zoning ordinance in addition to the soil maps that are also incorporated in the legal document.

It is the intention of staff planners to recommend a "Flood Plain Conservation District Ordinance" wherever appropriate when developing comprehensive plans.

In December 1964, the first Flood Plain Conservation District Ordinance in the county was adopted by Lower Salford Township. It is expected that two other townships will soon follow suit. The Lower Salford Ordinance places limitations on the use of soils affected by stream flooding and other structural problems. Under this ordinance, structures and on-site sewage disposal systems are prohibited in a Flood Plain District. The use of land "in harmony with the conservation" of these natural drainageways is encouraged. The ordinance was prepared under the advisement of the County Planning Commission and the Soil Conservation Service. Thus far very favorable reactions have been received from soil and conservation specialists throughout the country. In regards to the legality of the ordinance, lawyers have assured all concerned that it is legal in the mode and intent that it was written. One can only wait and see how the first test case comes out, when the ordinance has "its day in court."

The problem of preparing adequate soil maps for inclusion in the ordinances has been satisfied by two methods: (1) Supplying the municipality with positive prints of the soil field sheets and delineating the alluvial soil boundaries, and (2) Preparation of an uncontrolled aerial photo mosaic and, again, delineating the alluvial soil boundaries.

It was decided that any attempt to compile the alluvial soils on a base map for inclusion in the Ordinance would be foolhardy and might possibly weaken the legal stand of the document. When the official soil survey manual is available, most of the time-consuming methods now being utilized will be replaced by using the printed maps and accompanying text.

An interesting note on alluvial soils was reflected recently upon examining the 50-year flood plain data as defined by the

U.S. Army Corps of Engineers on a flood plain study of the Wissahickon Creek, a major tributary in the eastern part of the county. The alluvial soils, as indicated by the soil survey follow very closely this 50-year flood frequency.

PROPOSED ORDINANCES BASED ON SURVEY DATA

Presently, the Montgomery County Planning Commission is using the results of the soil survey to prepare two new model ordinances. One model will specify that areas of steep slopes be protected and preserved in accordance with the concepts set forth by zoning ordinances and comprehensive plans. The other model will specify that measures be taken to provide some form of agricultural zoning. Unfortunately, zoning is such in Montgomery County that all but two municipalities in the county have their own ordinances, hence, county zoning cannot be applied. The concept being followed is to have each municipality, where it is so willing, to adopt these newer ordinances according to their own needs.

SOIL SURVEY DATA AND THE COMPUTER

In the future, the county will consider applying advanced automated computer techniques to the soil survey data. These computer applications will result in the ability to translate graphical data into tabular and then the reverse. By utilizing an electronic coordinatograph and readout system, it will be possible to obtain area measurements and true positions of any desired data in a fraction of the time normally required.

THE SURVEY IN RETROSPECT

In retrospect, one can understand that the role of soil maps and their interpretations in planning for today and tomorrow is fundamental. The problems which now confront man are becoming more complex as our once vast resources of open space and rural elements of the land begin to diminish. The time for effectuating and implementing our soil surveys, our land use plans, and our comprehensive plans, is now at hand! They should be utilized and not just admired as impressive volumes of data among the many now occupying shelves veiled in the obscure dust of time. This can be brought about only through close coordination of public and private efforts, expanded interpretations, and widespread understanding.

Everyone has a share of the responsibility. What will you do with your share?

CHAPTER 4

USE OF SOIL MAPS BY CITY OFFICIALS FOR OPERATIONAL PLANNING[1]

W. R. Hunter,[2] C. W. Tipps,[2] and J. R. Coover[3]

THE CITY OF San Antonio, Texas, the home of the Alamo, has made extensive use of soil maps in both general and operational planning. Through cost-sharing agreement with the Soil Conservation Service the city obtained advance copies of soil maps and a soils handbook of the greater metropolitan planning area of San Antonio. Some additional soil investigations were made in the area. The additional investigations included characterization of the various soils as to (1) corrosivity to metal, (2) depth of soil to bedrock, and (3) character of the bedrock or the underlying materials to a depth of ten feet. The soil handbook describes the soils, gives their chemical and physical properties, including engineering properties, and gives soil interpretations important to the use of the soils.

The most extensive use of the maps has been in day-to-day operational planning. The City Public Service Board, the City Water Board (city-owned gas and water utilities), the Parks and Recreation Department, and the special projects engineer of the city use the soil maps most frequently.

DESIGN OF CORROSION CONTROL FOR PIPELINES

Past experience in the city with the design and performance of buried pipelines left much to be desired. A number of soil properties are known to affect the cost of installation and length of service. Shallow soil depth to hard rock directly affects costs of excavating trenches. Hard rock fragments or gravel in the soil and backfill material may bring about damage to protective pipe coatings. Shrink-swell properties of soils may preclude the use of rigid utility pipe construction materials.

---

1. Contribution from the City of San Antonio, Texas, and the Soil Conservation Service.

2. Special Projects Engineer, City of San Antonio, and Corrosion Engineer, City Public Service Board, San Antonio, Texas.

3. State Soil Scientist, Soil Conservation Service, USDA, Temple, Texas.

Some of the soil properties affecting corrosion of pipes are: (1) presence of excess soil moisture, (2) low electrical resistance, and (3) differences in drainage or soil permeability that cause differential aeration along a buried metal pipe. These properties in various combinations contribute to varying degrees of galvanic corrosion occurring on the outside of the metal pipe.

The engineer-designer may also contribute to the corrosion problem by burying connected dissimilar metals. The rate of dissimilar metal corrosion is affected by the soil properties previously mentioned.

Protection of pipelines from corrosion includes the use of protective coatings and cathodic protection. Sacrificial metals are buried and connected to the pipelines according to the degree of corrosion hazard. The City Public Service Board uses soil maps in designing the type and location of zinc or magnesium sacrificial anodes for corrosion control, which is known as cathodic protection. Zinc anodes are used for an approximate design life of 30 years, if soils have a resistivity of less than 1500 ohms per cubic centimeter. For soil resistivity values of 1500 ohms/cc and over, magnesium anodes must be used to obtain adequate corrosion control.

Since coating performance also is a prominent factor in corrosion control by cathodic protection, it is vital to specify adequate padding material in areas containing large gravel, flint rock or fragmented limestone. The soil map shows these areas.

Soil depth determines the specific location of anodes within the general area for which they are designed. Packaged zinc anodes are buried horizontally in deepened sections of the trench at a depth of approximately 18 inches beneath the pipe. Zinc and magnesium bar anodes are buried in 6-inch diameter bore holes extending to depths of 7 to 13 feet beneath the pipe. The anodes are connected to the pipe with a lead wire.

COST ESTIMATES FOR PIPELINE CONSTRUCTION

Soil maps are used in estimating the cost of installing underground utility lines, especially the cost of excavation. Generally the excavation is done at lowest cost with special trenching machinery. The speed at which such a machine operates will determine its cost efficiency. If rock is encountered so that blasting or air hammers must be used instead of ditching machines, an additional cost of $10 to $12 per cubic yard must be added. The City Public Service Board now has its own blasting personnel and equipment and uses soils information to augment experience in planning for future needs.

Contingent contracts are written to allow for additional rock excavation expense, or in some cases contracts for gas main extensions are based on 100% rock excavation. This use of the soil maps alone represents savings of thousands of dollars per year.

Without previous knowledge, sandstone float-rock may be completely overlooked in the southeast quadrant of the urban expansion. Every test hole drilled ahead of a recently installed 30-inch gas supply line missed every float-rock. Yet, the continuous trench intersected many such float-rocks 12 to 30 inches thick, requiring air hammers for excavation. This line was laid immediately prior to the completion of the soil mapping. Observation by soil scientists along the open trench showed the presence of the float-rock only in the parent materials of certain soils. The soil map is now used to predict the occurrence of these float-rocks.

GREENBELT PLAN

San Antonio has planned for the future a greenbelt encircling the City in the metropolitan area. In planning the greenbelt, extensive use was made of soil maps. The concept of the greenbelt is to utilize open space areas within the confines of the metropolitan boundary to break up the monotony of City structures. It was important to know the kinds of soil that would be encountered in order to design the area for use as parks, nature areas, agricultural purposes, drainageways, and right-of-way for utilities and streets. City planners, with the knowledge of the physical and chemical characteristics of the soils and their use suitability acquired from the soil maps and soil handbook, set the boundaries of the greenbelt. These boundaries were adjusted to include sources of construction material, stream beds, flood plains, and areas with high expansive soils that were more suitable for horitcultural practices than they were for foundations of structure.

Without the soil survey the project would have required many extra man hours of field work and the final design would have been subaltern. Planners have labeled the soil survey an invaluable tool for use in their profession.

PLANNING PARKS AND RECREATION FACILITIES

Parks are normally of four approximate sizes: neighborhood parks of 10 acres, community parks of 50 acres, area parks of 300 acres, and metropolitan parks of various sizes. Each type of park contains certain facilities that can be developed best on soils suitable for that use. A study of the soil map with the necessary interpretive information has shown that some sites can be more economically developed on fewer acres and be more desirable than other sites.

A recent problem of the Parks and Recreation Department was to locate a suitable site for a thousand-acre metropolitan park. A landscape architect and a special projects engineer were assigned to the problem. The problem was reduced to a detailed study of three sites. In comparing the three sites, items that were considered pertinent to soil characteristics were:

1. One million cubic yards of soil suitable for the construction of a runway at International Airport and suitability of the borrow pit for water storage for water-oriented sports
2. Soils suitable for lining bottom of borrow pit
3. Soils suitable for construction of earth fill dam
4. Local materials for constructing park roads, parking areas, boat ramps, beaches, and trails
5. Soils suitable for septic tank filter fields at restroom sites
6. Soils suitable for excavation for underground utilities
7. Soils suitable for grass and trees and irrigation systems
8. Soils suitable for foundations of structures

The use of the soil survey on the aerial maps along with the soil handbook made it possible to make an authentic comparison of the three sites with a minimum of field work.

At Southside Lions, a 320-acre park, the soil survey was invaluable in the design of a 10-acre lake and 2 miles of park roads. Most of the park was covered with thick and thorny brush and inaccessible for inspection. The soil survey indicated that the tops of three hills had an outcropping of caliche gravel. A trail was hacked to the tops of the hills and the sites proved to be caliche gravel of the finest grade for base material. An extra mile of park roads was built due to savings from finding the caliche pits on the site where base material could be hauled with scrapers instead of from distant pits with dump trucks.

A tennis center, consisting of 18 playing courts, rest rooms, concession building, and service street, was located and designed by using the soil survey. The decision to remove a high shrink-swell soil and replace it with caliche under the courts and parking areas was predicted on the soil information. The foundations for the buildings were designed to fit the soil conditions. The depth of fence and backstop posts in the ground was increased over the normal depth.

Two hundred and fifty acres were purchased adjacent to the

park. The soil maps showed Frio silty clay loam with gravel beds in some areas below depths of 6 to 15 feet. Expressways to be built in the vicinity would require several million cubic yards of embankment material to be borrowed at the most economical haul distance. This area proved to be economical and the material suitable. As a result, a 50-acre recreation lake will be built in the park.

DESIGN APPROVAL OF FOUNDATIONS FOR RESIDENCES

The local Federal Housing Administration office uses soil maps and the soil handbook in helping to determine the eligibility of residential subdivisions to receive guaranteed loans. They also use the information when checking foundation designs for individual residences. Soil interpretation maps showing three shrink-swell values as critical, marginal, and noncritical are constructed from information on the soil maps and used successfully to show the home builders the relation of the soil to the design of the slab-on-ground foundation.

The soil survey has many uses for builders and potential home owners and they should take advantage of the soil survey in purchasing land, designing the subdivision, and designing the foundations of the residences.

OTHER USES OF SOIL MAPS

A contractor's engineer used information from the soil survey to schedule excavation and site work on the construction of the Northside School Project. Soil several feet deep, was removed, stockpiled, and used to cover fill material obtained from excavation for the school building. The depth to rock shown in the test boring data made by engineers in their on-site study compared favorably with data in the soil handbook. This indicates further the predictive value of the soil maps and their interpretations for estimating the suitability of the soil for a building site.

Drainage engineers use the soil information to determine the run-off factor used in designing storm drainage structures and to determine the required back slope on open ditch storm sewers.

The City Water Board bases much selection of construction materials and methods on soil survey data.

SOME PROBLEMS IN USE OF THE SOIL MAPS

Graphic interpretation of the characteristics of the soil as related to a specific use in the form of interpretation maps have not been completed for the greater planning area of the city except that the City Public Service Board and City Water Board has graphically interpreted the soil characteristics as related to corrosion of underground utilities.

One of the greatest problems experienced with the use of the soil survey has been the lack of interpretive soil maps and the distribution of the soils information. Data are available for making the maps. It is just a matter of funds to finance the preparation of such maps. There are many architects, engineers, and planners who are not fully oriented on the use of the soil information. These people would use the soil information more readily if interpretive soil maps were constructed to fit their need and made available to them. The interpretive maps most useful in this area would be as follows:

1. Suitability of soils for home sites based on plasticity index and shrink-swell
2. Suitability of soils as source of sand and gravel
3. Suitability of soils for roads
4. Suitability of soils for growing trees
5. Relation of soils to surface run-off
6. Suitability of soils for cultivated drops, pasture, and range
7. Relation of soils to corrosion of underground conduits

CONCLUSIONS

The value of the soil maps and the soil handbook containing interpretations for the short period they have been available to the city of San Antonio has been proved by savings of time and money. Their use has resulted in improved designs, more effective planning, and more accurate preliminary estimates of construction costs. Elected and appointed officials in metropolitan areas, developers, and private citizens cannot afford to be without soil survey information.

CHAPTER 5

THE USE OF SOILS INFORMATION IN URBAN PLANNING AND IMPLEMENTATION

John G. Morris[1]

FUNDAMENTALLY, urban planning represents an effort to regulate the consumption of land and other natural resources such as air and water in the growth of the urban centers. However, just as the road to Hell is paved with good intentions, the road to urban chaos is paved with unexecuted plans. To be effective, plans must be implemented; otherwise they are nothing but good intentions. In this paper I shall discuss actual experiences in the use of soil maps to implement urban or metropolitan planning. Three specific situations will be discussed in which soil maps were used to implement urban plans.

First I want to emphasize the importance of soils information and its use by those involved in planning the growth and development of metropolitan areas.

Disposal of domestic sewage is quite commonly attempted through the use of on-lot soil absorption fields which, generally speaking, function as reverse drains or subsurface irrigation systems. When this is done without proper soils evaluation, dire consequences often follow. The basic problem is the soil on which the home and the septic tank filter field are constructed and this is the one component of the sewage disposal system which the builder cannot readily manipulate. The only solution to the problem is public sewers, and in many instances this is too costly. It is difficult and expensive to change the site for a building after it has been purchased. If the soil is poorly suited for the intended use, there is little that can be done without great expense to change it. In some instances one can design the structure to combat the limitations of the soil but the problem must be known prior to construction.

USE OF SOILS MAPS IN A COMMUNITY ACTION PROGRAM

My first illustration involves the use of soils maps in a community action program in a small municipality of approximately 400

---

1. Superintendent, Lake County Public Works Department, Waukegan, Illinois.

homes and containing about 2200 home sites. The lots were small—7,500 to 10,000 square feet. The area was platted prior to the existence of soils maps. The community has been plagued with a high incidence of septic tank failures. However, there was a reluctance by people in the community to accept the health department's recommendation based on percolation test results that the soils were inadequate. Inconsistent results and the uncoordinated method of making the percolation tests did not evoke support of the community's leadership. The sanitarian had nothing concrete on which to base his decisions as to suitability for on-site sewage disposal. One lot appeared to be adequate for on-site disposal and the next one was not adequate. Generally, the attitude was that septic tank failures were an individual problem and that if the residents would just treat it right they wouldn't have any trouble. The general attitude was one of indifference mixed with hopelessness or confusion.

Following the availability of soil maps and interpretations for use in this area it was possible to tie the individual problems together and show that the problem was truly a community problem that could not be effectively solved through an individual approach. The soils in this community fall into two categories: those that are predominately marginal for use in soil absorption sewage disposal systems and those that are considered to be poor to unsatisfactory. On the former the county health department has a record of 8 existing failures of soil absorption fields and on the latter the department has a record of 35 failures.

The use of soils maps made it possible to demonstrate that continued development on small lots would result in additional failures because the soils are not satisfactory for on-site disposal of sewage. On the basis of soils information a strong recommendation was made that a community sewer system was the proper solution to the community's sewage disposal problems. The soil map was something that people could see and understand. It provided a logical explanation for those areas where septic systems failed and where they functioned properly.

My second illustration involves the use of soils maps in the acquisition of open space. In this instance the Lake Bluff Park District used soils maps as evidence in condemnation proceedings to support their valuation of the property involved. The land being condemned was in a high priced estate type development located in a north shore community bordering on Lake Michigan. The Park District introduced soils information in the form of a soils map prepared by the Soil Conservation Service, USDA, in cooperation with local and state agencies to back up its claim that the soils involved in the condemnation were not stable enough to support building foundations in certain locations. It was further pointed out that extensive improvements involving drainage and undercutting would have to be made before the land could be subdivided. In view of this fact the value of the land was considered significantly below the value of adjoining land suitable for subdividing in its present state.

In addition to the soils information, the attorney for the Park District introduced evidence as to the location of high water in the area and notes recorded on a plat of survey made in 1924 delineating the limits of what were described by the surveyor at that time as low wet lands. It is of interest to note the close agreement between these completely unrelated sources of information, the modern soil map and the survey made in 1924, regarding the character of the lands involved. Recurring high water generally reaches elevation 670. The limits of Houghton mulch generally follow the 670 contour and the limits of low wet lands as defined by the surveyor in 1924 were between the 669 and the 672 contour. In this instance the significance of the soils map was that it showed the extent of the undesirable soils whereas a single or a limited series of soil borings does not have this dimension.

The attorney for the condemnee rebutted the Park District's testimony with soil borings and an engineer's interpretation which developed the argument that the soils were suitable for building provided certain precautionary measures were taken. The Park District's attorney did not engage in extensive cross examination nor did he subject the soils expert to redirect examination.

I would be leaving you with a false impression in this instance if I did not provide you with the opinion of the Park District attorney regarding the use of soils maps as evidence in condemnation cases. The attorney, as a result of his experience, advised me that presently soils maps alone in his opinion do not make desirable evidence from an attorney's standpoint. His reason for this is that it is too vulnerable to the challenge of accuracy. He states that the court is not familiar with the procedure involved in making a soils map and as a result direct examination of the witness is necessary to lay the foundation for using the soils information. In addition, there are a number of people involved in the preparation of a soils map and this too presents an added difficulty for an attorney wishing to present the soils map as evidence. He did state, however, that the soils map was very good evidence in the case involved.

The map served to support the low valuation of the property involved. It further strengthened the other evidence introduced, that of high water and the 1924 survey report.

The attorney concluded with a summary statement that the soils map was probably most effective in that it provided added information relating to the suitability of the soils involved for building foundations and other uses incidental to subdividing. The attorney recommended that soil scientists stay very close to attorneys for condemnors such as highway departments, park districts, forest preserves and other public agencies having the power to condemn land. Only by acquainting the court with the techniques involved in making soils maps and through repeated use of thie information as evidence in condemnation proceedings will this weakness of being subject to challenge for reasons of accuracy be eliminated.

USE OF SOIL MAPS IN DEFENSE OF ZONING

My third example involves implementing a plan the hard way. One of my cynical friends once advised me that securing compliance with the law was not so much a matter of education as to the soundness of the law but rather a matter of education to the fact that the law is effectively enforced. While I may not entirely agree with this, the practical fact of the matter is that once a law is circumvented many others may try the same procedure. This case involves an attempt to rezone 80 acres of property downward from 5-acre zoning to 1-acre zoning on the basis that the county's 5-acre zoning in the area was not a proper use of the land. The county defended its position that the zoning was in conformity with adjoining land use which was primarily estates.

It is again an exclusive area of high priced homes and very low-density development. The developer presented testimony from a professional engineer that the soil was suitable for on-site sewage disposal systems on lots of 1 acre. Precolation tests certified by the engineer varied from 15 to 60 minutes per inch and averaged about 30 minutes per inch. The engineer's note describing the soil stated that it was a light brown clay sand and silt mixture to the bottom of an 8-foot-deep test hole and that there was no water standing in the hole after three days. The date on the engineer's report is given as December 29, 1962. The county health department, at the request of the county's attorney, attempted to perform percolation tests in the same area on February 18, 19, and 20, 1963, and could not do so in six of nine locations because of the fact that ground water infiltrated into the percolation test holes and flooded them. In three other locations percolation rates averaged about 120 minutes per inch. Information from a soils map was overlayed on the proposed 1-acre zoning plat to clarify the contradictory position of the developer's consulting engineer and the county health department's findings. It was rather obvious that percolation tests by themselves alone would have been of no help in this situation. By combining the percolation tests results with the soil map the county was able to resolve the apparent contradiction and strengthen its argument that the soils were unsuitable for on-site sewage disposal on 1-acre tracts. To further its point the county introduced a sketch plat which showed how zoning with 5-acre lots can provide proper distribution of soils so that more desirable soils for on-site sewage disposal may be found, thus avoiding the creation of unsatisfactory conditions.

Again in this instance there was some controversy between attorneys as to the reliability of soils map information. However, the county was allowed to present the soils map partly because the soil scientist that made the map was still located in the country. Had he not been available we may not have been able to introduce the soils map as evidence. I believe this echoes the feelings of the attorney for the Lake Bluff Park District who stated that presently soils map information is very susceptible to a challenge based on accuracy. As stated earlier, it is not a matter of accuracy of the maps but one of establishing in the courts the manner in which they are made and precedence that the courts have accepted them as sound, accurate information germane to the problem.

In addition to the above examples, over the past three years Lake County officials have been actively using soils map information in working with developers of large subdivisions. Many of these are subdivisions of over 160 acres in size. In all of these instances the subdivider and the county have both benefited through the development of a better plan representing better use of the land and more effective implementation of the county's land use plan through the use of soils map information.

People who are acquainted with the value and use of soils maps should make a concerted effort to reach local officials in their community responsible for planning and implementing the community's growth and development to urge them to use soils map information as an additional tool. It will be a difficult and tedious process and there is a great inertia to overcome but in the long run it will be worth it. We have so little of our heritage of land and water resources left in our metropolitan areas that it behooves us to use it wisely.

CHAPTER 6

APPLICATION OF SOILS STUDIES IN COMPREHENSIVE REGIONAL PLANNING

Kurt W. Bauer[1]

THE POPULATION of the United States is presently undergoing an unprecedented growth and urbanization. Nationally we are concentrating our population in about 200 large metropolitan areas. Yet, within these metropolitan areas we are decentralizing our population, thereby spreading urban development out across city, county, and even state boundary lines. Under the effects of this urban diffusion, entire regions, such as southeastern Wisconsin, are becoming mixed rural-urban areas. This is, in turn, creating a host of new and intensified areawide development problems of an unprecedented scale and complexity.

The problems encountered in providing economically feasible facilities for importing, diverting, and transporting potable water, sewage, and storm drainage, for controlling pollution of streams and lakes, ground water, and air, and for providing safe and rapid air and surface transportation for these large urban regions are, even when considered individually, some of the most complex problems facing our society. These problems, moreover, are all closely linked to far more basic problems of land and water use, and are thereby inextricably interrelated. The formulation of sound solutions to these problems, therefore, requires a comprehensive, areawide approach, an approach which we in southeastern Wisconsin have chosen to call regional planning.

Such an approach must recognize the existence of a limited natural resource base to which both rural and urban development must be properly adjusted in order to ensure a pleasant and habitable environment. Land and water resources are limited and subject to grave misuse through improper land use and public facility development, misuse which can lead to severe environmental problems. In such a regional planning effort, then, the selection of desirable areawide development plans from among alternatives must be based in part upon a careful assessment of the effects of each particular

---

1. Executive Director, Southeastern Wisconsin Regional Planning Commission, Waukesha, Wisconsin.

42

alternative plan on the supporting natural resource base.

Such emphasis on the natural resource base is essential if better regional settlement patterns are to be evolved and irreparable damage to limited and increasingly precious land and water resources avoided. Such emphasis, however, requires the collection and analysis of a great deal more information concerning the natural resource base and its ability to sustain rural and urban development than has been collected before in major regional or metropolitan planning operations. Such information includes definitive data on surface and ground water resources, woodlands and wetlands, fish and wildlife, existing and potential scenic, historic, scientific, and recreational sites, and on soils.

NEED FOR SOILS STUDIES

Soil properties exert a strong influence on the manner in which man uses land. Soils are an irreplaceable resource, and mounting pressures upon land are constantly making this resource more and more valuable. A need exists, therefore, in any comprehensive regional planning program to examine not only how land and soils are presently used but how they can best be used and managed. This requires an areawide soil survey which shows the geographic locations of the various kinds of soils, identifies their physical, chemical, and biological properties, and interprets these properties for land use and public facilities planning.

For planning application, the necessary soil suitability study should be designed to permit preliminary assessment of:

1. The engineering properties of soils as an aid in the development and selection of desirable spatial distribution patterns for residential, commercial, industrial, agricultural, and recreational land use development;
2. The soil-plant relationships for agricultural and nonagricultural uses, including natural wildlife relationships, as an aid in the selection of desirable spatial distribution patterns for permanent agricultural and recreational greenbelts and open spaces;
3. The suitability and limitations of soils for engineering applications, such as private on-site sewage disposal facilities, agricultural and urban drainage systems, foundations for buildings and structures, and water storage reservoirs and embankments as an aid in the planning and preliminary design of specific development proposals and in the application

of such plan implementation devices as zoning, subdivision control, and official mapping;

4. The engineering properties of soils as an aid in the selection of highway, railway, airport, pipeline, and other transportation facility location; and
5. The location of potential sources of sand, gravel, and other mineral resources.

Such an areawide soil suitability study is not intended to and does not eliminate the need for on-site foundation investigations and laboratory testing of soils for the final design and construction of specific engineering works. Such a study provides a means of predicting the suitability of land areas for various uses and thereby to permit, during the planning stage, the adjustment of regional settlement patterns, broadly considered, to an important element of the natural resource base.

Historically, the study of soils has been directed primarily to single-purpose applications, and little attention has been given to soil potentials on a comprehensive, areawide basis. Particularly, the study of soils has been historically related to use for agriculture and forestry, with little attention given to the ways in which soil properties might influence urban uses of land.

PROCEDURE

Standard soil surveys, such as those conducted by the Soil Conservation Service, U. S. Department of Agriculture, in cooperation with the state agricultural experiment stations, however, if accompanied by appropriate interpretations can be adapted to meet the basic soils data needs of comprehensive regional planning programs. These surveys are made by carefully examining the soil in its natural state and delineating areas of similar soils on an aerial photograph. The areas so mapped are keyed to a national classification system, in which all soils identified as belonging to a given series have, within defined limits, similar physical, chemical, and biological properties, these properties being determined by field and laboratory tests. This makes it possible to predict the behavior of the mapped soils, based upon past experience with similar soils, under any proposed land use. These surveys have certain limitations particularly with respect to depth surveyed and with respect to the possible inclusion of soils with slightly different properties within mapped areas, because of map scale, time and cost limitations. Nevertheless, these surveys represent the best available source of areawide soils information today. The surveys are carried out by experienced soil scientists and constitute a valuable basic scientific inventory which, if accompanied by the necessary interpretations, has multiple planning and engineering uses.

REGIONAL PLANNING IN SOUTHEASTERN WISCONSIN

An example of a comprehensive regional planning program emphasizing a comprehensive assessment of the effects of alternative development patterns on the natural resource base is that of the Southeastern Wisconsin Regional Planning Commission. The Commission is the official planning and research agency for one of the large urbanizing regions of the nation and exists to serve and assist the local, state, and federal units of government in planning for the orderly, economic development of the seven-county Southeastern Wisconsin Region.

Regional planning as conceived by the Commission is not a substitute for, but a supplement to, local planning. Its objective is to aid in the solution of areawide development problems which cannot be properly resolved within the framework of a simple municipality or single county. As such, regional planning has three principal functions:

1. Areawide research, that is, the collection, analysis, and dissemination of basic planning and engineering data on a continuing, uniform, areawide basis, so that the various agencies of government, private enterprise, and interested citizens within the region can better make decisions concerning community development;
2. Preparation of a framework of long-range plans for the physical development of the region, these plans being limited to those functional elements having areawide significance;
3. Provision of a center for the coordination of the many planning and plan implementation activities carried on by the various levels and agencies of government operating within the region.

The work of the Commission is visualized as a continuing planning process providing many outputs of use throughout the region, outputs of value to the making of development decisions by public and private agencies and to the preparation of plans and plan implementation programs at the local, state, and federal levels.

Reliable basic planning and engineering data collected on a uniform, areawide basis is absolutely essential to the formulation of workable development plans. Consequently, inventory becomes the first operational step in any planning process, growing out of program design. The crucial importance of factual information to the planning process should be evident since no intelligent forecasts can be made or alternative courses of action selected without knowledge of the current state of the system being planned.

The sound formulation of regional plans or major plan components, therefore, requires that factual data must be developed on:

1. The existing land use pattern;
2. The potential demand for each of the major land use categories and the major determinants of these demands;
3. The existing local development objectives and constraints;
4. The underlying natural resource base and the ability of this base to support land use development;
5. The existing and potential demand for transportation, utility, and public facility services within the region and on the major determinants of these demands; and
6. The existing and potential supply of transportation, utility, and public facility system capacities.

The data must be developed through major planning inventories; and these inventories, when considered together, must be comprehensive, encompassing all the various factors which influence and are influenced by regional growth and development. Each inventory must be in a form which permits any finding to be related to the whole. The data collected in the necessary inventories must be pertinent to describing the existing situation with respect to regional development and identifying existing problems with respect thereto, forecasting future land use and public facility requirements, formulating alternative development plans, and testing and evaluating such alternative plans.

One of the most important of such basic data inventories carried out under the Commission work program concerns the soils of the region. At the time of the creation of the Southeastern Wisconsin Regional Planning Commission, a very limited amount of useful data on the soils of the region was available. General soil maps, which show broad soil groupings at a small scale and provide limited interpretations for agricultural purposes, had been completed at various times in the past for each of the seven counties comprising the 2,689-square-mile region. Modern standard soil surveys covering approximately 38 percent of the region, but again accompanied by only agricultural interpretations, had also been completed in connection with the preparation of basic farm conservation plans. In addition to being directed primarily at agricultural land use and treatment, these surveys had a further limitation in that they covered scattered farms rather than broad areas.

On the basis of this prior work, however, it was established that soils having questionable characteristics for on-site sewage disposal were widespread throughout the region. It was estimated that approximately 40 percent of the soils occurring within the region possessed severe limitations in this respect. Urban development undertaken in disregard of these soil conditions had actually created severe environmental problems within the region, with the result that restrictions had been placed by the State Board of Health on the development of new subdivision plats in certain areas of the region. It was further estimated that in some portions of the region lying within the immediate path of urbanization up to one-third of the area might be covered by soils with severe limitations for intensive urban development, even if served by public sewers. Tests performed by the U. S. Bureau of Public Roads and the State Highway Commission of Wisconsin on selected soil samples also reflected the questionable adequacy of many soils within the region as a foundation for transportation system structures.

The region, moreover, lies within a wholly glaciated area; and this glacial history has created highly complex soil relationships and an extreme variability and intermingling of soils within even very small areas. The usefulness of generalized soils maps for definitive planning purposes within the region was, therefore, severely limited. The widespread occurrence of soils having questionable characteristics for certain types of urban development, coupled with the glacial history of the area, indicated the need for detailed soils surveys as an absolute prerequisite for sound areawide development planning. Moreover, adequate soil suitability data were found necessary to the application of both a regional land use simulation model and a land use design model being developed by the Commission as a part of its land use-transportation planning program. The amount of land within each U. S. Public Land Survey section suitable for various types of urban land use was a necessary input to these models, and it was determined that this essential input could not be properly provided without data from a detailed soil survey.

In order to fulfill the soils data requirements of the regional planning program, a cooperative cost sharing agreement was negotiated for the completion of modern standard soil surveys of the entire region (2,689 square miles) together with the provision of interpretations for planning purposes. Specifications governing the work were drawn by the Commission staff and were incorporated in the interagency agreement. These specifications called for some kinds of information not normally provided in soil surveys and contained the following salient provisions.

Mapping and Photography

Base maps prepared by the Commission under its initial planning program, and recent (April 1963) vertical aerial photographs prepared under the land use-transportation planning program, both covering the entire region, were to be used as base maps and the soil survey. In order to assure full compatibility with other Commission work, maximum utilization of these base maps and photographs in the conduct and presentation of the work was specified. Specifically, all new standard soils mapping was to be done on ratioed and rectified aerial photographs prepared from Commission negatives utilizing Commission base maps for horizontal control.

Operational Soil Survey

Standard soil surveys (detailed operational soil surveys) were to be completed for all those areas of the region not previously so surveyed (estimated at approximately one million acres) and such surveys were to be carried out in conformance with the latest standard operational procedures of the National Cooperative Soil Survey as set forth in the U. S. Department of Agriculture Soil Survey Manual. Boundaries of soil mapping units were to be identified on prints of aerial photographs, prepared in accordance with the Commission specifications as already noted, and all mapped soil areas identified by a suitable legend. Field mapping was actually accomplished, in accordance with the specifications, as a scale of 1" = 1320' (1:15840), each field sheet consisting of a ratioed and rectified vertical aerial photograph covering an area of six square miles (six U. S. Public Land Survey sections). All previously completed standard soils mapping was transferred to such current photography, in order to provide uniform coverage of the entire region. The Commission was furnished, on a work progress basis, with reproducible half-tone negatives of the completed field sheets, prepared in accordance with the specifications of dimensionally stable cronar base material at a scale of 1" = 2000' (1:24000), to match the scale of the Commission base maps. These reproducible negatives are suitable for the preparation of inexpensive prints by diazo process and clearly show the soils mapping with delineations and identifying symbols so that the prints may be used for planning and engineering purposes on a work progress basis, not only by the regional planning staff, but also by state and local governmental agencies and private investors.

Finished photo maps, at a scale of 1" = 1320' (1:15840), again utilizing negatives provided by the Commission, are to be prepared to accompany the standard published soil survey of the U.S. Department of Agriculture. Each such finished photo map is to cover an area of six square miles (six U. S. Public Land Survey sections). Key planimetric features, such as highways, railroads, streams, lakes, cemeteries, and major structures are to be identified on the finished photo maps as are the U. S. Public Land Survey township, range, and section lines.

Soils Data and Data Interpretations

A report will be made available immediately upon completion of all the field mapping in the region. It will contain the information necessary to utilize the soil survey data in plan preparation and implementation at both the regional and local level. This information will include definitive data on soil properties and interpretations of these properties for planning and engineering purposes. Thus, each kind of soil within the region will be rated in terms of the inherent limitations for specific land uses and engineering applications. Soil interpretations will include:

1. Potential agricultural uses, including soil capabilities for common cultivated crops, crop yield estimates, woodland suitability groups, and crop adaptation;
2. Wildlife-soil relationships, including capability of the different kinds of soil to sustain various food plants and cover for birds and animals common to the area;
3. Non-farm plant material-soil relationships, including suitability of different kinds of soil for lawns, golf courses, playgrounds, parks and open space reservations;
4. Soil water relationships by kinds of soil, including identification of areas subject to flooding, stream overflow, ponding, seasonally high water table, and concentrated runoff; and
5. Soil properties influencing engineering uses, including depth to major soil horizons important in construction, liquid limit, plastic limit, plasticity index, maximum dry density, optimum moisture content, mechanical analysis, AASHO and Unified classifications, percolation rate, bearing strength, shrink-swell ratio, pH, depth to water table, and estimated depth to bedrock if within approximately 20 feet of the ground surface.

Interpretations of these data for planning purposes are also to be provided, including:

1. Suitability ratings for potential intensive residential, extensive

residential, commercial, industrial, transportational, natural and developed recreational, and agricultural land uses;

2. Suitability ratings for septic tank disposal field, building foundation for low buildings, trafficability, surface stabilization, road and railway subgrade and earthwork uses;

3. Suitability ratings for use as a source material for road base, backfill, sand or gravel, topsoil and water reservoir embankments and linings;

4. Ratings with respect to flooding potential, watershed characteristics, susceptibility to erosion, and susceptibility to front action; and

Table 1. Selected measured, and estimated chemical and physical properties of soils of southeastern Wisconsin.

Soil number, type & horizon		Classification			Mechanical analysis, % passing sieve†		Maximum dry density lb./cu.ft	Optimum moisture content	Permeability, in./hr.
Symbol	Depth, in.	USDA texture	Unified	AASHO	No. 10, 2.0 mm	No. 200, 0.07 mm			
217, Bono silty clay loam									
A	0-12	si. cl. l.	MH	A-7	100	100	107	18	0.2-0.8
B	12-36	si. cl.	CH	A-7	95	95			0.2-0.8
C	36+	si. cl.	CH	A-7	95	95	109	18	0.05-0.2
297, Morley silt loam									
A	0-12	si. l.	ML	A-4	100	85	98	25	0.8-2.5
B	12-36	si. cl.	CH	A-7	100	95			0.2-0.8
C	36+	si. cl. l.	CL	A-6	100	90	120	14	0.2-0.8
299, Blount silt loam									
A	0-10	si. l.	ML	A-4	100	85	98	25	0.8-2.5
B	10-36	si. cl.	CH	A-7	100	100			0.2-0.8
C	36+	si. cl. l.	CL	A-6	100	95	120	14	0.2-0.8

		Percolation rate, min/in	Liquid limit	Plasticity index	Shrink-swell potential	Bearing strength	Reaction (pH)	Depth to water table, feet	Susceptibility to erosion
A	0-12	120-300	55	30	High	Poor-low	6.6-7.3	‡	A-slight
B	12-36	120-300			High	bearing	6.6-8.5		
C	36+	300+	38	22	High	capacity	7.4-8.5	0-1	
A	0-12	31- 60	56	32	L-M§	Poor-low	5.6-7.0	3-5	A-slight
B	12-36	61-120			High	bearing	5.6-7.0	>5	BMCN-mod.
C	36+	61-120	27	12	Mod.	capacity when wet	7.4-8.5		DKEF-severe
A	0-10	31- 60	56	32	L-M§	Poor-low	5.6-7.3	0-2	A-slight
B	10-36	61-120			High	bearing	5:6-7.3		B-mod.
C	36+	61-120	27	12	Mod.	capacity when wet	7.4-8.5	3-5	

* All three soils are moderately susceptible to frost action, have low bearing strength, and a depth of more than 5 feet to bedrock. Variations in these properties would be shown in additional columns of the table. † 100% of all samples passed No. 4 sieve (4.70mm). ‡ Seasonal. § L = Low, M = Moderate.

Table 2. Suitability rating* of soils of southeastern Wisconsin for rural and urban land use development.

Soil type and number	For agri-cultural use	Residential development			Commercial and industrial development	Trans-porta-tion systems
		With public sewer	Without public sewer			
			Less than one acre	One acre or more		
76 Will Loam	Fair Good when drained (Poor for trees)	Poor	Very poor	Very poor	Good when drained	Poor
217 Bono Silty Clay Loam	Good when drained (Poor for trees)	Very poor	Very poor	Very poor	Poor	Poor
297 Morley Silt Loam	Good on 0-6% slope, Fair on 7-12% slope (Fair for trees)	Good	Question-able	Poor	Fair on 0-6 % slopes, Poor on slopes over 6%	Poor
298 Ashkum Silty Clay Loam	Good for crops when drained, Good for pasture, (Poor for trees)	Very poor	Very poor	Very poor	Poor	Poor
299 Blount Silt Loam	Good for crops when drained, Good for pasture (Fair for trees)	Fair	Very poor	Question-able	Poor	Poor
398 Ashkum Silt Loam	Good for crops when drained, Good for pasture (Poor for trees)	Poor	Very poor	Very poor	Poor	Poor

* Suitability rates apply to entire soil profile and its position in the landscape.

Table 3. Suitability ratings and limitations of soils of southeastern Wisconsin for specific engineering purposes.

Soil type and number	Limitations for		Suitability as a source of		Corrosion potential	
	Road subgrade	Foundation for low buildings	Topsoil	Sand & gravel	Metal	Concrete
217 Bono Silty clay	Very poor	Very poor	Good-sur-face, Very poor-subsoil	Very poor	Very high	Low
297 Morley Silt Loam	Poor	Fair	Good-sur-face, Poor-subsoil	Very poor	Mod-erate	Low
299 Blount Silt Loam	Very poor	Poor	Good-sur-face, Poor-subsoil	Very poor	Very high	Low

5. Suitability for wildlife habitat and habitat improvement, lawns, golf courses, playgrounds, and parks and related open areas requiring the maintenance of vegetation.

All of the data collected and all of the interpretations are to be summarized in tabular form suitable for ready use in planning and engineering analyses. (See Tables 1 through 5.)

Utilization of Soils Data

In the application of soils data, the planner is concerned not only with the properties of the various soils and the interpretation of

Table 4. Suitability rating* of soils of southeastern Wisconsin for recreational development.

Soil type and number	Play-grounds, parks, and picnic areas	Bridle paths and nature and hiking trails	Golf courses	Cottages and utility buildings	Camp sites	Remarks
76 Will Loam	Poor	Poor	Poor	Very poor	Very poor	Suited to wildlife and ponds, High water table
217 Bono Silty Clay Loam	Poor	Poor	Poor	Very poor	Very poor	Suited to wildlife and ponds
297 Morley Silt Loam	Good on 0-2% slopes, Fair on 3-6% slopes	Good on 0-12% slopes, Fair on slopes over 12%	Good on 0-6% slopes, Fair on 7-12% slopes	Poor	Good on 0-6% slopes, Fair on 7-12% slopes, Poor on slopes >12%	
298 Ashkum Silty Clay Loam	Poor	Poor	Very poor	Very poor	Very poor	Suited to wildlife and ponds
299 Blount Silt Loam	Fair	Fair	Fair	Poor	Poor	Seasonally high water table, Subject to ponding
398 Ashkum Silt Loam	Poor	Poor	Poor	Very poor	Very poor	High water table, Suited to wildlife and ponds

* Suitability rating applies to entire profile including subsoil and substratum; suitability rating for all other use considers entire soil profile.

Table 5. Suitability ratings, limitations, and selected properties of the
soils of southeastern Wisconsin for watershed management purposes.

Available water capacity, in./in.	Flooding potential	Irrigation potential	Suitability for reservoir embankments and linings
0-10 - .2 10-36 - .18 36+ - .16	Subject to ponding	Poor	Good to fair impervious Medium to low stability & high volume change
0-10 - .2 10-36 - .18 36+ - .16	None	Fair-A,B & M slope Poor- C & N slope Very poor- D,E & F slope	Good to fair impervious Low stability & large volume change
0-10 - .2 10-36 - .18 36+ - .16	Subject to occasional ponding or flooding	Fair at A & B slope	Good to fair impervious Low stability & large volume change

these properties in terms of suitability for various land uses, but
also with the spatial distribution of the various soils, their areal
extent and their location with respect to other factors influencing
regional development, such as existing land uses, utility service
areas, accessibility patterns, and transportation service levels and
areas.   Moreover, the necessary soils information may be used
either graphically, as for example, to show how soils having various
properties are distributed relative to each other, to other elements
of the resource base, and to existing land uses; or quantitatively, as
for example, to determine the total area covered by soils having
certain properties. Therefore, the soils data resulting from the detailed operational soil surveys must be adapted for ready use in the
regional planning program. This requires appropriate transformation of the soils maps and interpretive data into the two forms in
which it is actually used: graphic and numeric.

The soils information converted to graphic form has application
in any planning operation involving the spatial location of uses on
the land. An example of such an operation is the preparation of a
regional land use plan by conventional planning techniques. In this
application, areas covered by soils poorly suited to each of the various land uses are delineated on planning base maps so that these
areas may be avoided in the spatial distribution of proposed land
uses during plan synthesis. In this way, the detailed operational
soils survey provides a new input into traditional plan synthesis operations and makes these traditional techniques far more powerful
and effective. Other planning operations in which the soils data has
been applied in graphic form in southeastern Wisconsin include the
preparation of zoning district maps, the design of detailed neighborhood unit development plans, the design of subdivision layouts, and
the preparation of site plans. The graphic data has also been used

in subdivision plat review, tax assessment, and development financing. Other uses readily suggest themselves in resource development and management, as well as in other functional areas of planning.

In order to permit the efficient application of the soils data in graphic form, the Commission staff is preparing interpretative soils maps. These maps are being prepared at a scale of 1" = 2000' (1:24000) by county as overlays to the Commission base maps and will be reduced for publication at a scale of 1" = 4000' (1:48000). The interpretative maps are being prepared for seven kinds of potential land use: (1) agricultural, (2) large lot residential without

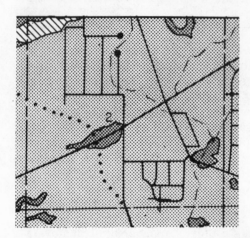

INTERPRETATIVE SOILS MAP
FOR AGRICULTURAL USE

Symbol	Suitability Rating
[ ]	Very Good
[ ]	Good
[ ]	Fair
[ ]	Poor
[ ]	Questionable
[ ]	Very Poor

INTERPRETATIVE SOILS MAP
FOR LARGE LOT RESIDENTIAL
USE WITHOUT PUBLIC SANI-
TARY SEWER SERVICE

Figure 1. Interpretative soils maps for agricultural and large lot residential uses.

public sanitary sewer service, (3) small lot residential without public sanitary sewer service, (4) residential with public sanitary sewer service, (5) industrial, (6) transportation route location, and
(7) intensely developed recreational. Each interpretative map will
show the six soil limitation ratings: very slight, slight, moderate,
severe to very severe, and very severe. (See Figures 1 through 4.)
These terms are defined as follows:

1. Very slight: little or no soil limitations, very good suitability for use;
2. Slight: slight soil limitations, easy to overcome during development, good suitability;

INTERPRETATIVE SOILS MAP
FOR SMALL LOT RESIDENTIAL
USE WITHOUT PUBLIC SANI-
TARY SEWER SERVICE

Symbol	Suitability Rating
	Very Good
	Good
	Fair
	Poor
	Questionable
	Very Poor

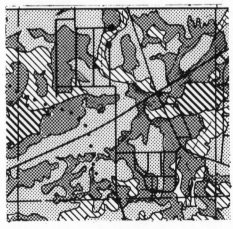

INTERPRETATIVE SOILS MAP
FOR RESIDENTIAL USE WITH
PUBLIC SANITARY SEWER
SERVICE

Figure 2. Interpretative soils maps for small lot residential use without public sewer service and for residential use with public sewer service.

3. Moderate: moderate soil limitations can be overcome with careful design and good management, fair suitability;
4. Severe: severe soil limitations, difficult to overcome during development, poor suitability;
5. Severe to very severe: very severe soil limitations, very difficult to overcome, require detailed on-site investigations, questionable suitability;
6. Very severe: very severe soil limitations that lead to serious construction and maintenance problems, very poor suitability for use.

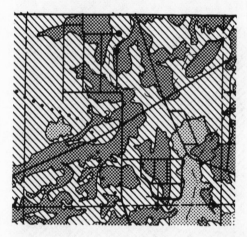

INTERPRETATIVE SOILS MAP
FOR INDUSTRIAL USE

Symbol	Suitability Rating
	Very Good
	Good
	Fair
	Poor
	Questionable
	Very Poor

INTERPRETATIVE SOILS MAP
FOR TRANSPORTATION ROUTE
LOCATION

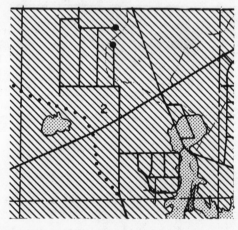

Figure 3. Interpretative soils maps for industrial and transportation route uses.

APPLICATION OF SOILS STUDIES

In addition, a slope map will be prepared for each county us
the following slope ranges: 0 through 1%, over 1 through 5%, over
through 8%, over 8 through 11%, over 11 through 14%, over 14
through 19%, over 19 through 29%, and over 29%. Other interpretative maps for planning and engineering purposes based upon quantitative soil properties readily suggest themselves and can be prepared as the regional planning work progresses to more definitive
phases.

Quantification of Mapped Data

The soils data converted to numeric form has application in any
planning operation involving mathematical computation and analysis.

INTERPRETATIVE SOILS MAP
FOR INTENSELY DEVELOPED
RECREATIONAL USE

Symbol	Suitability Rating
	Very Good
	Good
	Fair
	Poor
	Questionable
	Very Poor

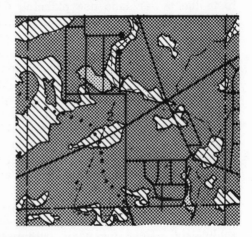

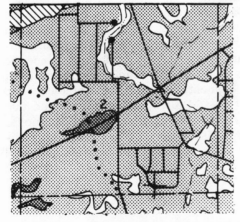

SLOPE MAP FOR PLANNING
AND ENGINEERING PURPOSES

Symbol	Percent of Slope
	0 — 1
	2, 3, 4, 5
	6, 7, 8
	9 & Above

Figure 4. Interpretative soils map for intensely developed recreational
use and slope map for engineering purposes.

ch an operation is the determination of weighted
noff. Such determination permits the soils data to
d in storm sewer design and thereby permits a
ement in existing design techniques. Another ex-
ication of the soils data in numeric form is in the
~~~~~~~~~~~~~~ or developable land area acreage figures. Such application greatly expedites the quantification of land use planning data
and the achievement of a balanced allocation of land to the various
uses which meets the land use demand growing out of the social,
economic, and physical needs of the region and is at the same time
properly related to the natural resource base.

The most important application of the numeric data, however,
is in the newer land use planning techniques, which utilize mathematical models in the synthesis of land use and community facilities
plans. Both the land use design model, being developed by the Commission to synthesize land use plans, and the land use simulation
model, being developed by the Commission to test land use plans,
require detailed operational soils data in numeric form for their
operation. Indeed, such soils data provides the essential link between development costs and geographic location inherent in the
construct of the models and essential to their application.

In order to permit the efficient application of the soils data in
numeric form, the soil mapping units are being measured by U. S.
Public Land Survey Section using random sampling techniques, and
the percentage and total areas of each of the various soils within
each section so determined, coded, and transferred to punch cards
for processing, tabulation, and use in planning analyses and model
application. Once the basic data is on punch cards, the percentage
and total areas of each of the various suitability groupings within the
region and any subareas of the region, such as watersheds, planning
districts, or traffic analysis zones, can be determined by machine
methods. Even more important, however, is the fact that once the
soils data are on punch cards they can be readily correlated with
other factors influencing development, the data for which can also
be stored on punch cards. It should always be remembered that
soils are only one of the factors influencing development decisions.
Therefore, this correlation of soils data with other essential planning data by machine methods is an extremely important and useful
advantage.

SUMMARY AND CONCLUSION

The regional planning program in southeastern Wisconsin represents a unique effort to relate the preparation of areawide urban

development plans to the natural resource base so that future development problems and accompanying deterioration of the regional environment may be avoided. Need exists in such a comprehensive regional planning program to examine not only how land and soils are presently utilized but also how this resource can best be used and managed. This requires an areawide soil suitability study which shows the geographic locations of the various kind of soils, identifies their physical, chemical, and biological properties and interprets these properties for land use and public facilities planning. The resulting comprehensive knowledge of the character and suitability of the soils is one of the most important tools through which an adjustment of areawide urban development to the supporting resource base can be accomplished and is extremely valuable in every phase of the planning process. Soils information can comprise important inputs into the formulation of goals and objectives, the preparation of planning standards, the analysis of existing land use, plan synthesis, test, and evaluation, and, perhaps most important of all, plan implementation. In southeastern Wisconsin the solid information is comprising important inputs into the regional land use-transportation planning program, into watershed planning programs, and into the community planning assistance programs presently underway.

Moreover, detailed operational soil survey data can, if properly applied, provide the basis for many important day-to-day community development decisions by federal, state, and local units of government and by private investors. Definitive soils data are essential to intelligent zoning, subdivision control, and official mapping at the local level of government, just as such data are essential to the preparation of a regional land use plan, a regional transportation plan, a comprehensive watershed plan, or an intelligent farm conservation plan. Since the soil surveys represent a basic scientific inventory, they provide valuable information needed for the planning, location, and design of highways, parks, land subdivisions, and sewage disposal facilities, as well as for agricultural and forest land use planning and management.

If soil properties as revealed by a detailed operational soil survey are ignored during either general or detailed plan formulation, not only will expensive obstacles to plan implementation occur, but irreparable damage may be done to the land and water resources of the community. A detailed operational soil survey, therefore, is one of the soundest investments of public funds that can be made.

CHAPTER 7

USE OF SOIL SURVEYS BY A PLANNING CONSULTANT

Carol J. Thomas[1]

A PRIVATE PLANNING CONSULTANT is a trained planner who serves governmental units concerned with physical growth and development. He does for the community or governmental unit what you do in your own life when you assess your assets and goals, budget and plan for the future. He may specialize in some aspect of planning, as schools or transportation, and then assist city or other planning staffs with these problems, or he may specialize in general planning for a community or political unit which cannot afford a planning staff.

The planning with which he assists includes preliminary studies or fact finding, general land use planning, and planning for municipal facilities to serve the various areas and types of land use. These facilities include streets, utilities, schools, parks, dumps, cemeteries, forests, police stations, fire stations, and all other services and structures which are in the public domain. Planning also includes implementation of plans—for example, zoning by-laws, subdivision regulations, and capital budgeting.

Although planning is a municipal function dating from biblical days, its importance is accentuated today, when we are in the midst of a population explosion. The population of the country has increased almost 10% since 1960 and will have almost doubled the 1960 population by the year 2000. This growth puts tremendous demands on towns—for example, each 100 new families means 100 more acres of private land in use and 4 more acres of public land in use, 4 classrooms, 40,000 gallons of water a day, 15,000 feet of streets. It is because of this terrific demand on resources that I will direct most of my remarks to how the consultant uses the soil study to develop a general land use plan to accommodate growth in towns.

A general land use plan is the portion of a comprehensive plan or guide for the growth of a community that deals with the allocation and distribution of land use throughout the community. The types of land use included residential areas of various density,

---

1. Community Planner, Cochituate, Mass.

by which is meant number of people per acre. They also include commerce, industry, agriculture, recreation and extractive industries, water, transportation, utilities, and open space. Since the plan indicates the location, amount, and sometimes the intensity of each use, it establishes the character of a community, the pattern of civic, economic, and human life. It aims to minimize travel time between home and work or other activities, to provide a pleasant environment free of nuisance, to assure a healthy en—vironment, and to minimize the economic strain of community development.

Many factors influence the development of a plan: The raw materials, the labor market, the location and circulation patterns, to name a few. However, in a given situation there may be no precise decision or compelling determining factor to affect a choice among possible uses. A hillside might look attractive and thus be designated a single-family residential area, although it could as easily have been used for attractive office sites, garden apartments, or permanent open space. In this instance as in many others, a decision by a professional or a town board of laymen may well have been reached by intuition, common sense, or political pressure.

Because of such problems, the planners have long been seeking a means to remove or to verity some of the intuitive aspects of planning. They also needed a tool of some scientific worth to assist in resisting political pressure. Thus we are joining the engineers and sanitarians who make use of data the soil scientist can provide—not in the micro-analysis of an individual parcel or building site, as do the other professions, but in terms of general conditions which may affect larger areas.

Cost sharing arrangements can be made whereby a community can acquire soil survey maps and interpretations for general or operational planning purposes. The soil survey for general planning includes three items: A grouping of all the soils into associations, each composed of somewhat similar soils; a brief description of each association, including suggested uses of the land of the association; and a map of general soil ssociations. The following is one such description written for the ᵢayman.

Paxton-Woodbridge Association: <u>well-drained and moderately well-drained, stony and bouldery soils underlain by hardpan on</u> 3 to 35% slopes.

This association occupies 29% of the town. It is most prevalent in the northern portion. The terrain is made up of dome-shaped hills with steep slopes. Much of the association is in

woodland. Farming is also an important land use. Most of the
orchards are in this association. Paxton soils occupy 70% of
the association and Woodbridge soils, 30%.

Paxton soils are well-drained fine sandy loams underlain by
firm galcial till. Hardpan is present at a depth of 2 feet.
(This is a fact important to the planner.) Nearly a third of
the Paxton soils occupy slopes steeper than 25%; few occupy
slopes less than 8%. Woodbridge soils are moderately well-
drained fine sandy loams underlain by firm glacial till. Hardpan is present at a depth of about 2 feet. Woodbridge soils
occupy slopes of 3 to 8% in the lower portions of hillsides.
Included in the associations are the well-drained Essex and
moderately well-drained Scituate soils. They are like the Paxton
and Woodbridge soils, except for being somewhat sandier. (Note:
the layman can understand such a description.)

The soils of this general soil area are among the best for
agricultural and woodland uses. They hold ample moisture
during the normal growing season and leaching losses are slight.
Surface stones have been removed from some tracts to facilitate
tillage. The soils present problems when used for commercial,
industrial, or high-density residential purposes where community sewage disposal is not available. The hardpan restricts
water from moving downward readily. When the soil above the
hardpan is saturated, water tends to move downslope along the
top of the hardpan. Hardpan layers have slow to very slow
permeability and individual sewage effluent disposal systems do
not function satisfactorily. This general soil area may be expected to yield sufficient groundwater for home use. However,
the yield is usually not sufficient for commercial, industrial,
or municipal uses.

Plate 3 on page 183 shows a typical general soils map for a
small community with about a half dozen associations. I have
rather arbitrarily selected the Town of Stow, Massachusetts, as
an example from the many communities for which we have used
soil surveys in our planning work. As in this case, soil associations generally run from very poor soils (Muck-Scarboro) to
those more suited to urban use.

The soil descriptions and the map provided by soil scientists
must be translated to a plan. This is the planner's task. First,
we interpret the soil descriptions for planning purposes. Table 1
shows a summary of such an interpretation. The table includes
information on the following items:

Name of soil association

Table 1.   Interpretation of soils report for appropriate
zoning use classification and soil type.

General soil areas	Major characteristics	Best use	Secondary use		Recommended lot size		
			Type	Correction	No service	Water only	Water & sewer
1. Paxton-Hollis	11% of town; well drained, very stony bedrock, hardpan-2', 3-15% slope	woodland wildlife recreation	agriculture, low-density residence, medium-density residence	remove stones, public water, water & sewer	-	40,000 sq. feet	20,000 sq. feet
2. Ridgebury-, Peat-Muck-Whitman	15% of town; poorly drained R-hardpan, 14" P-M-water table near surface W - hardpan 14" saturated	wildlife woodland recreation	not feasible	drainage expensive, difficult foundations, (supports light loads only)	-	-	-
3. Paxton-Woodbridge-Ridgebury	72% of town; hardpan-18-24" slow permeability	woodland	agriculture, residential uses, industry business	remove stones, public sewer, public sewer and water	-	40,000 sq. feet	20,000 sq. feet
4. Merrimac-Walpole-Agawam	3% of town Sand and gravel at 2'	commercial, industry,residence, woodland,wildlife,recreation	agriculture	irrigation & fertilizing	40,000 sq. feet	20,000 sq. feet	15,000 sq. feet

Most appropriate land use
Corrections necessary for other uses
Appropriate lot size, if any, with no public service or water;
  with public water and sewer; with public water, sewer, and
  storm drainage
Suggested kind of land cover
Suggested percent of the land that can be used for different
  purposes and in different ways

These are the interpretations made by a planner and reviewed
by the soil scientist.

Secondly, we work with the soil map to further subdivide or group the soils into areas which are not buildable, those which are buildable with corrective measures, and those which are readily buildable. Table 2 shows the kinds of data we assemble for this interpretation. Map 1 shows vacant buildable land map.

Table 2. Appropriate residential area per dwelling unit.

Soil Type	Description	Best Use	Corrective Measures- Other Uses	Drainage Characteristics	Limita- tion	Best Land Cover	% of Land Coverages

Appropriate Residential Area Per Dwelling Unit					Approx. Lot Width and Yard Requirement	Scoring Weight
No Services	With Water	With Sewer	With Water & Sewer	With Water, Sewer & Storm Drainage		

Third, the soils which are buildable or which are buildable with corrective measures are subject to further study. As noted on the table for residential uses, appropriate lot sizes are determined for areas to be served with sewer, storm drainage, and water, with one service only, or in some instances without either water or sewers. The appropriate lot size for each major kind of soil based on available services is dependent on the following factors:

Soil permeability - will a cesspool or septic tank function? How much area does it need? How long will it function?
Ground water supply - is there likely to be enough for home site supply? (The sample description of Paxton-Woodridge indicated it was adequate.)

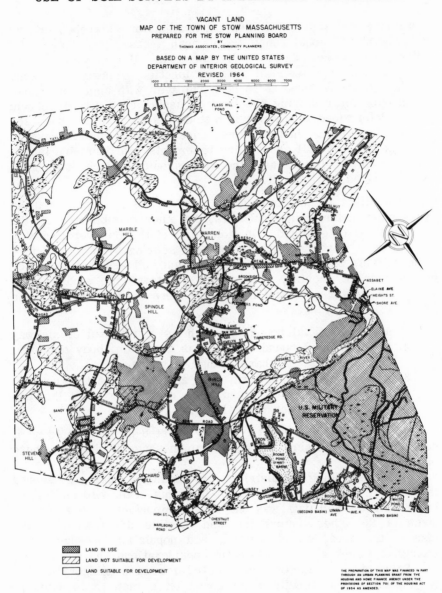

VACANT LAND
MAP OF THE TOWN OF STOW MASSACHUSETTS
PREPARED FOR THE STOW PLANNING BOARD
BY
THOMAS ASSOCIATES, COMMUNITY PLANNERS

BASED ON A MAP BY THE UNITED STATES
DEPARTMENT OF INTERIOR GEOLOGICAL SURVEY
REVISED 1964

LAND IN USE
LAND NOT SUITABLE FOR DEVELOPMENT
LAND SUITABLE FOR DEVELOPMENT

THE PREPARATION OF THIS MAP WAS FINANCED IN PART
THROUGH AN URBAN PLANNING GRANT FROM THE
HOUSING AND HOME FINANCE AGENCY UNDER THE
PROVISIONS OF SECTION 701 OF THE HOUSING ACT
OF 1954 AS AMENDED.

Map 1. Vacant land map of the Town of Stow.

Hardpan and lateral seepage - will wastes invade the water supply, or otherwise pollute the area? Will basements be wet or flooded? Will foundations be endangered from lateral seeping and freezing?

<u>Drainage</u> - design water disposal system for watershed to take care of additional runoff from urban areas.

<u>Hardpan and water table</u> - will basements fill with water? Will on-site sewage disposal systems function properly? If sand and gravel removal is to be permitted, with applicable safeguards for restoring the land to usable condition, it should be determined in advance if that use is for building purposes or recreation. In the former case, removal must cease at a height that will assure dry basements and operative facilities. In the latter case, the level should be such that ponds, if desired, will result.

In addition to determining the appropriate lot size for those areas planned for residential uses, the other feasible uses of the land must be determined. In Volume II of the Hanover Report a first attempt was made at developing a scoring system to determine suitable uses of major soils in each soil association. For convenience of scoring, we divided the town into study areas. Wherever possible, evident boundaries were used. Some of these are:

1. Major artificial boundary, such as a railroad or highway
2. Major natural boundary, such as a stream, body of water, ground cover, or sharp change in grade
3. Existing land use pattern, such as the demarcation between built-upon and vacant land, or a change in type of land use as from residence to business.

Occasionally no evident boundary existed so that we found it necessary to use discretion and common sense in drawing these bounds.

After describing the districts for working purposes, we scored these areas for possible land uses in terms of the information we had acquired. Soil data was one of the important factors scored. Some of the other factors included tangible items such as the size of the area, street pattern, and population pressures and intangible items such as aesthetic considerations and tax return.

Each of these factors was scored for each category of use on a table. The results were coded on a map to be used in determining the general land use plan and in preparing recommendations for land uses, i.e., conservation areas, low, medium, high density residence, business, and industry.

Though use of soil data in general land use planning is intended to be positive, the use of the scored data developed starts with a negative approach. Areas suitable only for conservation, etc., not for any type of building, habitation, or agriculture, are placed in such a category first. The land which is marginal or capable of correction for certain uses is then considered and these areas are systematically categorized for use on the basis of soil limitations and other scored factors. Thus, by working from the most restrictive usage, based on the kinds of soil, to the least restrictive or unrestricted use, an attempt is made to create a land use pattern such that all land within a particular recommended district is satisfactory for that use from a soil criteria standpoint while also satisfactory on the basis of other planning criteria.

This was indeed an elementary and arbitrary scoring system. We are now progressing so that we can provide the soil scientist with better planning criteria and have him tell us suitable uses or corrective measures needed for various uses for the different kinds of soil.

If full services (water, storm sewers, and sanitary sewers) are provided and the soil is suitable for residence, the soil is usually suitable for business and industry. The common exception is based on slope, undesirable for commercial uses, which may be turned to a residential advantage. Another exception is when the soil will not support heavy weights. In this case, after all other planning factors are examined, if this soil association or parts of it seem likely areas for business or industry, the decision is one of economics—is it worth pilings, floating foundations or whatever other corrective measure may be required for soils with low bearing strength. All adverse soil conditions can be surmounted if the economic pressure is great enough, as in the case of Manhattan or Back Bay in Boston.

Where full services are not provided, the suitability for commercial and industrial purposes is a bit more difficult to ascertain. Uses which require a large supply of water or which have large wastes to dispose of can usually be eliminated from consideration. In all other cases, it is a matter of not exceeding the density permitted for residence. For example, if you have determined that acre zoning is appropriate where you have neither water or sewer, and you have predicted 3.5 persons per dwelling unit, you would have a proposed density of 35 persons per 10 acres. Assuming these people are there two-thirds of the day and gone a third for school or work—admittedly an over-simplification—and assuming that the business or industry would only have personnel present one-third of the day, the business or industry on the same type soil could be permitted a concentration of 70 persons per 10 acres. In addition, the larger type of on-site disposal systems which they would require would need approval. The density control device can also be used for consideration of the appropriateness of garden apartments or cluster zoning. The soil may make it impossible for on-site facilities to function when the development is concentrated or may lead to a disruption of the water table or flooding of basements.

Once the appropriate use for each kind of soil is determined, it is not a matter of simply transferring the soil boundaries to a general land use map coded for the appropriate use. In the first place, consideration must be given to the juxtaposition of the different kinds of soil. Returning to our example of Stow, there are instances of the very suitable soil association 1 being jeopardized by association 2. The extreme slope of No. 2 causes such rapid run-off in some areas that No. 1 cannot accommodate it, and temporary wet spots will result. These may not show up at the time of examination for building sites or percolation tests, so the proposed land use plan must be drawn carefully to minimize uses which can be harmed by this happenstance.

In the second place, consideration must be given to other planning factors. The present land use pattern and economic pressures are, of course, paramount.

Let us look at Stow's present land use, Map 2, and then at the land use plan, Map 3.

The core of the plan is the town center, where the location of all civic uses plus local shopping and parks is planned. The ring around the center core is an area for medium density residence - an area convenient to the center and its services and an area to be served by water. (Major recreation facilities can be provided in this ring and the center core through maximum use of town facilities and development of Wheeler Pond.)

The plan is flexible. In the low-density or rural areas, uses other than residences are permitted, provided that a site plan is approved and provided that rigid requirements for, among other things, landscaping, parking, control of noise, glare, and other objectionable features are met. In no case of such private development are more people permitted to congregate than are permitted to be assembled on the land for residential purposes.

Other features of the plan include permission, with restrictions, for various type of residence, designation of neighborhood business areas, protection of the Assabet River and adjacent lands, including an outstanding pine forest, green strips, and protection of areas for future development as neighborhoods.

Where the land use map indicates lands used at greater densities than the soil study indicates as feasible, we must look for

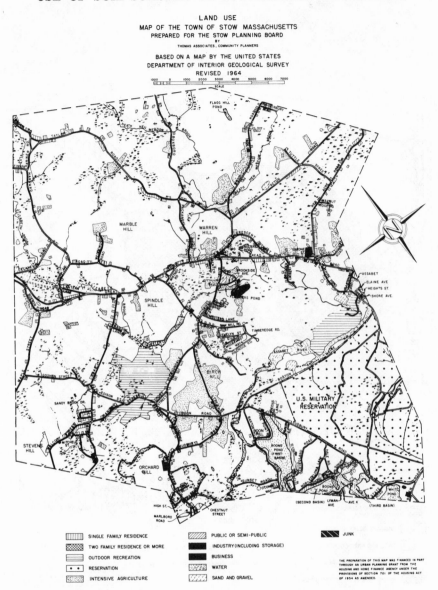

LAND USE
MAP OF THE TOWN OF STOW MASSACHUSETTS
PREPARED FOR THE STOW PLANNING BOARD
BY
THOMAS ASSOCIATES, COMMUNITY PLANNERS

BASED ON A MAP BY THE UNITED STATES
DEPARTMENT OF INTERIOR GEOLOGICAL SURVEY
REVISED 1964

	SINGLE FAMILY RESIDENCE	PUBLIC OR SEMI-PUBLIC	JUNK
	TWO FAMILY RESIDENCE OR MORE	INDUSTRY (INCLUDING STORAGE)	
	OUTDOOR RECREATION	BUSINESS	
	RESERVATION	WATER	
	INTENSIVE AGRICULTURE	SAND AND GRAVEL	

THE PREPARATION OF THIS MAP WAS FINANCED IN PART
THROUGH AN URBAN PLANNING GRANT FROM THE
HOUSING AND HOME FINANCE AGENCY UNDER THE
PROVISIONS OF SECTION 701 OF THE HOUSING ACT
OF 1954 AS AMENDED.

Map 2.   Land use map of the Town of Stow.

problems already existing or in the making.   These may be polluted wells, water in the basement, inoperative cesspools or septic tanks, excessive run-off.   In these instances corrective measures must be taken.   These measures may involve municipal

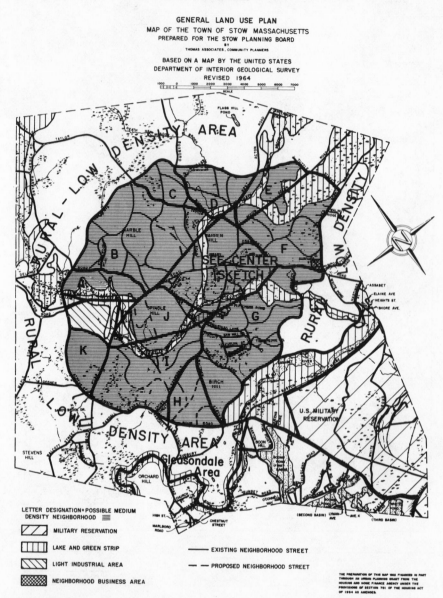

GENERAL LAND USE PLAN
MAP OF THE TOWN OF STOW MASSACHUSETTS
PREPARED FOR THE STOW PLANNING BOARD
BY
THOMAS ASSOCIATES, COMMUNITY PLANNERS

BASED ON A MAP BY THE UNITED STATES
DEPARTMENT OF INTERIOR GEOLOGICAL SURVEY
REVISED 1964

LETTER DESIGNATION= POSSIBLE MEDIUM
DENSITY NEIGHBORHOOD

MILITARY RESERVATION

LAKE AND GREEN STRIP

LIGHT INDUSTRIAL AREA   ——— EXISTING NEIGHBORHOOD STREET

NEIGHBORHOOD BUSINESS AREA   — — PROPOSED NEIGHBORHOOD STREET

Map 3.   General land use map of the Town of Stow.

sewer and water systems. These systems, plus existing land use patterns, may indicate a higher density than the soil conditions alone indicate. A careful analysis may indicate how long the municipality can postpone installation of services without serious problems.

The degree to which a soils map and its interpretations can be followed varies with the community involved. We have used as our illustration a town with much vacant land on the fringe of a metropolitan area.

Economic pressures are generally a more decisive factor in urban areas or areas subject to great growth. Where the need to use the land is so great that almost any cost seems justifiable to the private investor, soil data has two applications. It can be applied to the individual site involved to determine construction problems or to establish corrective measures; or it can be used by the planner to assure maintenance of green areas where these are appropriate.

In less-developed areas, whether or not the economic pressures are already acute, soil maps and interpretations can be used to assure orderly development of the town with orderly extension of municipal services. Let me illustrate this with two plans for very different communities we have proposed based in large part on the soil study. The first case is that of Williamstown, a delightful college town with the urban part of the town nestled in a valley in the Berkshire mountains. At first glance the mountains look like a beautiful area for low-density residence, although this would be in conflict with long-range plans of the state to keep the Taconic Ranges in their natural state or of all groups interested in maintenance of open space and preservation of the watershed. Just the desire of the town to have green spaces or to avoid the costs of pumping water up the mountains and plowing and maintaining mountain roads is not sufficient reason in Massachusetts to prohibit building. The unsuitability of the land for residence due to the inability to maintain sanitary facilities and the decided suitability of the land for other purposes, however, gives us the basis of our plan. The dominant soils are Nassau, shallow to bedrock, and Dutchess, a deep, well-drained soil.

Thus we proposed the soils in the Nassau association, primarily in the mountains, for a recreation-conservation district with the exception of areas in close proximity to existing street frontage. (See Map 4.) At the other end of the scale, we found the town established on some of the poorest soil - the town had already felt the consequences of this and built a sewer system. Therefore, in the center areas, where both water and sewer are provided, the greatest density is permitted except, of course, where flooding may occur. The next ring outward served by water is planned for a density that can get by without sewer for 10 or 20 years but not much longer. The next area of residence

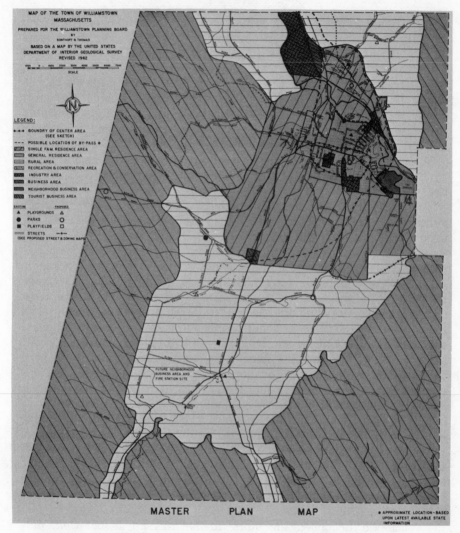

Map 4.   Master plan map of Williamstown, Massachusetts.

is predicated on a lot size that can survive almost indefinitely without sewer.

In the second case, Rowley, we are dealing with a coastal town with large tidal flats. The value of these flats to fish is now fully recognized, and there is a strong economic justification to prohibit encroachment on the flats. In the past, there had been some camps built on the flats, to which water was carried, and the wastes of which began to pollute the flats. Map 5 shows the general land use plan for Rowley.

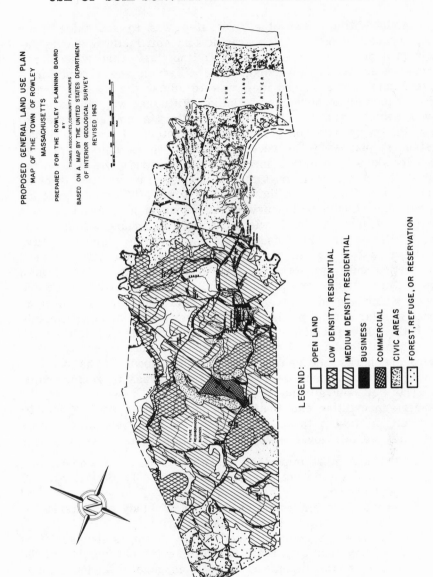

PROPOSED GENERAL LAND USE PLAN
MAP OF THE TOWN OF ROWLEY
MASSACHUSETTS

PREPARED FOR THE ROWLEY PLANNING BOARD
BY
THOMAS ASSOCIATES, COMMUNITY PLANNERS
BASED ON A MAP BY THE UNITED STATES DEPARTMENT
OF INTERIOR GEOLOGICAL SURVEY
REVISED 1963

LEGEND:

OPEN LAND
LOW DENSITY RESIDENTIAL
MEDIUM DENSITY RESIDENTIAL
BUSINESS
COMMERCIAL
CIVIC AREAS
FOREST, REFUGE, OR RESERVATION

Map 5. Proposed general land use plan for the Town of Rowley, Massachusetts.

As in Williamstown, the first step was to set aside lands that, because of peculiar topographic and soil factors, should remain in a permanent open state. To the flats were added lands primarily suited for woodland, most of which are already in a state forest. The second step was to adjust the feasible densities to municipal services. Unlike Williamstown, an extended sewer system was not planned, as Rowley is not anticipated to have the same type of growth or character. Instead, a small system is planned to correct a problem where soils have been used too densely over too many years - presently the land in the center is not servicing on-site systems and raw sewage is being dumped into a stream in the center of town. When this practice ceases, the stream will provide the nucleus of a pleasant park in the town center. Again, Rowley with only 16 square miles is unlike Williamstown with 45 square miles, and it is planned to have municipal water for all the buildable areas of the town. There are needed only two lot sizes then - one for the center of town where full services are available and one for the outer buildable areas, which are in this case composed of only two soil associations, similar enough so that one lot size can be selected suitable for both. The problem here is the fingers of unsuitable land. For general land use planning, we are utilizing these as green strips and parks between potential neighborhoods. The problem is more difficult when we translate these areas to zoning maps.

The soil survey and interpretation is a new tool for the planner—an exciting one to those of us who have worked with it. However, in taking these initial steps in the systematic use of soil data, we are governed by several limitations:

1. Perhaps most important, the need to curb our enthusiasm, so that we do not consider soil the only determinant of land use;
2. The lack of any established school of study or criteria for scoring soil data for land use determination;
3. The need for additional soil data. In any soil association you may find a parcel that differs in character from the whole, so that when you move from general land use planning, which we are discussing in this paper, to specific site analysis or development. For detailed planning you need detailed soil maps that show the individual kinds of soil in areas as small as two acres in size.
4. The need for more study and information. For example, although we have standards for how much park land we need per thousand persons, we do not know how much open

space we need per "anything" (people or acres) to preserve the balance of nature, to assure an abundant water
supply, or to prevent water pollution. This too may vary
by kinds of soil and the uses planned for the different
soils.

We use soil data for many things other than land use planning. They include subdivision design, on-site sewage disposal,
cemetery location, dump location, utility plans, building codes,
site development, domestic water supply, and recreation plans.

Soil surveys pay for themselves many times over. Proper
lot size determination alone may obviate the need for costly extension, saving millions of dollars. The soil survey has become
so important to us that we include it with the basic research we
do prior to initiating a plan.

CHAPTER 8

USE OF SOIL SURVEYS IN SUBDIVISION DESIGN

John R. Quay[1]

PROBLEMS ASSOCIATED with the application of the traditional gridiron system of land development are causing designers to seek a different approach to subdivision planning. Urban interpretations of soil surveys are being used to create subdivisions which take into account the capabilities of the land and which harmonize with the natural setting.

An examination of the original plan for the city of Philadelphia shows a gridiron of streets and blocks superimposed on land situated between two rivers. Topography and surface drainage have been ignored by the plan.[1]

Examples of grid development can be found in many of our American cities. Miami, Seattle, Chicago, and parts of Boston have superimposed the grid system on land forms differing greatly from each other.

One of the reasons for the prevalence of the gridiron pattern can be found in the survey system that has been used throughout much of the nation. The congressional township survey subdivides much of America into six-mile squares. These townships are further subdivided into square miles, or sections, which are in turn broken up into halves, quarters, eighths, etc.[4] This division by 2 is continued until the size is an odd number of acres, 5. At this point any further subdivision by 2 involves fractions of acres. Perhaps this is the reason we have so many 5-acre city blocks.

The 5-acre block, or some variation of it, is often the basic module of the gridiron system of subdivision. When local building and zoning restrictions are applied to this type of subdivision, we find that building areas become a uniform arrangement of parallel and/or perpendicular lines. Examining this type of subdivision with land use in mind, we find that approximately 30% of the area is used for streets and alleys, 10% for front yards, and the remaining 60% is available for building sites and side and rear yards. Depending on local customs and requirements, these

---

1. Architect, Barrington, Illinois.

figures vary from community to community. However, it is not uncommon to find one-third of the developed land area of a city devoted to streets and alleys.

In a sense, the gridiron system has been, and to a large degree still is, the essence of subdivision design. Today we tend toward squarer lots. We put curves in the streets, create larger blocks, sometimes labeling these "super-blocks," but underneath all of these contemporary trappings, much of our basic thinking is geared to a gridiron block system.

Fortunately, it is a rare case where the grid has not been interrupted or modified. An examination of the street and subdivision pattern of a section of land in most of our metropolitan areas will show that there has been some interruption and modification of the system.

In our core cities and in the inner ring of suburban communities we often find that neighborhoods composed of one or two sections of land have passed through an era of fashionableness and then started down the road toward urban decay, often becoming undesirable areas long before the man-made facilities have served a reasonable life expectancy. The reasons for this are many and varied - some involve the social, economic, political, and religious aspects of our society. Others deal with the natural and aesthetic environment.

In coping with this problem of deteriorating neighborhoods, many efforts, often termed "neighborhood conservation programs," have been and are being activated. The goals of these programs involve repair as well as removal. Inevitably, changes in land use result. More often than not, we find that land formerly used for dwellings, streets, stores, or factories ends up in some form of open use - parks, schools, playgrounds, parkways, etc.

The scheme developed by the Chicago Planning Commission and included as part of their "Basic Policies for a Comprehensive Plan of Chicago-1964" [3] is an example (Figure 1). However, even in programs such as this, the old, established gridiron still dominates. The only way significant change in physical platting can take place is through some form of public or quasi-public acquisition of large areas of land and complete rebuilding of the area.

The grid pattern is not just a problem of the core city. We find it in the small town and the suburban community.

A case in point is a subdivision on the south edge of the village of Barrington, Illinois (Figure 2). This subdivision was platted in the early 1920's when the village was a small rural community of a few hundred people. The north half of this

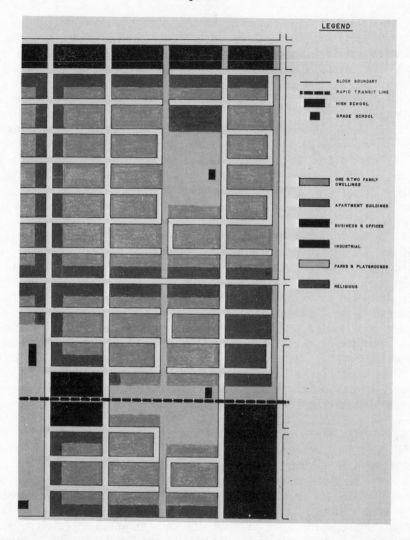

LEGEND

━━━━━━━ BLOCK BOUNDARY

■■■■■■■ RAPID TRANSIT LINE

██ HIGH SCHOOL

█ GRADE SCHOOL

███ ONE & TWO FAMILY DWELLINGS

███ APARTMENT BUILDINGS

███ BUSINESS & OFFICES

███ INDUSTRIAL

███ PARKS & PLAYGROUNDS

███ RELIGIOUS

Figure 1. Theoretical redesign of a square-mile section of Chicago showing proposed land use.

subdivision has developed into a stable residential area, while the south half has languished for more than 40 years with little or no development taking place.

When the subdivision plat is overlayed with a soils map on which urban capabilities interpretations are shown, this is easy to understand. (See Plate 4, page 184.) For the most part the soils in the north half are suitable for typical urban uses, while

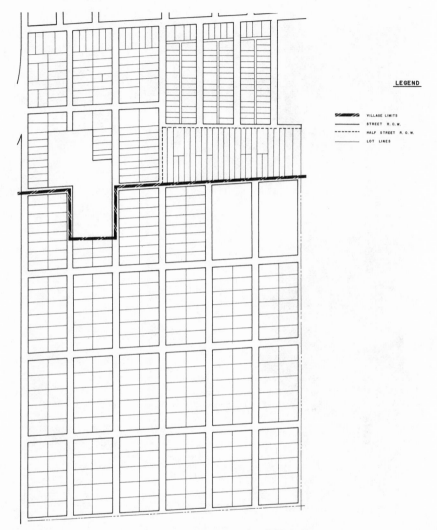

LEGEND

VILLAGE LIMITS
STREET R. O. W.
HALF STREET R. O. W.
LOT LINES

Figure 2.   Grove Street subdivision.

those in the south half tend to be marginal or definitely unsuitable for residential use.

This subdivision was not of the type that is common today in which the developer functions as both subdivider and builder. The subdivider functioned only as a land speculator, acquiring the raw land, subdividing, and then selling only the land. The land use map of the subdivision (Figure 3) was prepared by the village planners in 1958.[7]   It is interesting to note that where the

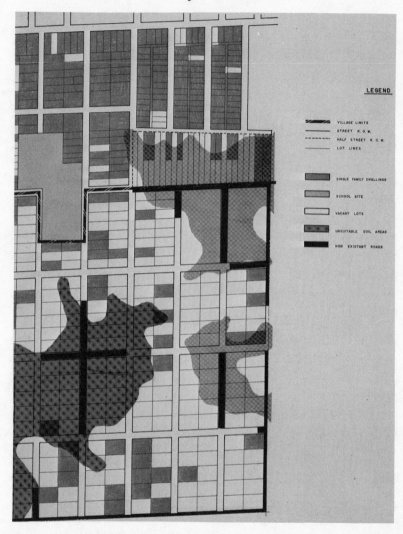

Figure 3.   Grove Street subdivision land use.

decision to build was left to individual lot owners they often had
the wisdom not to build on problem soils.

Maybe there is another approach to land subdivision besides
the T-square and slide rule technique.

Soil maps, with urban capability interpretations, often show
that all parts of any prescribed land area do not have equal potential for typical urban development. (See Plate 5, p. 185.)   If
the soil properties are studied, evaluated, and interpreted with

the idea of designing the urban development to conform to the capabilities of the land (See Plate 6, p. 185) rather than to arbitrary lot dimensions or to a rigid uniform grid, we will always achieve an urban environment that is harmonious with the natural physical environment. This produces urban surroundings which take advantage of nature instead of obliterating it. (The schemes shown in Plate 6 are arbitrary and consider only soil capabilities. The usual planning factors, transportation, utilities, economic feasibility, zoning, etc., have been assumed. The schemes are not shown as proposed plans, but for illustration purposes only.)

I have found the following procedure useful in applying the soil map and its varying interpretations in subdivision design.

Local subdivision regulations usually require that a topographical survey be included as one of the platting exhibits. By superimposing soil survey information on the topographical survey, a site evaluation map is developed. (See Plate 7, p. 186.)

The next step involves the charting of statistical data. [5, 6] (See Plate 8, p. 187.) Each soil is listed by name, number, and acreage. [8] Technical descriptions, horizons, and their depths are shown.

The task then becomes one of selecting the individual interpretations that are important to the specific project under consideration. The example shown is a 33-acre, low-density residential subdivision without public sewer or water facilities. Of the 75 or 100 possible interpretations, not all will be required. In the example shown, surface stabilization with additives, pH values, or depth to bedrock are factors of no immediate concern. (Bedrock in this area is about 200 feet below the surface.) The soil's ability to serve as reservoir or embankment lining had already been evaluated and used by the conservationist in developing the farm ponds. If the ponds had not already been constructed these interpretations might have been necessary design considerations.

The soil scientist in collaboration with the designer selected the interpretations pertinent to the problem. The soil interpretations selected were: 1-percolation rate; 2-flood potential; 3-water table; 4-bearing strength; 5-corrosion potential; 6-shrink-swell; 7-A.A.S.H.O. ratings; 8-erosion potential; 9-frost action; and 10-agricultural capabilities.

In this case, additional interpretations considered helpful but not essential were the suitability for: 1-trees; 2-shrubs; 3-grasses; and 4-wildlife.

All of the ratings, values, etc. for these interpretations were then charted. This produced a chart with numbers, letters, value ranges, etc., informative to the soils specialist but with very little meaning for representatives of other professions.

In bridging this communications gap, working with soils specialists,* I have developed a color coding system which we have found to be exceptionally helpful.

The soils scientist is able to categorize his data with varying degrees of refinement. Some interpretations require only three or four categories while others are broken into six or seven groups. The classic agricultural land use capabilities classification consists of eight classes.

Utilizing the idea oft the stop-light, we selected three colors, Green, Yellow, and Red, to represent: A. Proceed; B. Proceed with caution; and C. Stop - Danger.

We then selected three shades of each of these base colors to represent different kinds of soil limitations within the base grouping. We then had nine subgroups into which soil characteristics could be placed. We used green colors to represent soils with no problems or only minor, easily controlled problems, yellow colors to represent soils which present major but still controllable problems, and red colors to represent soils with major and/or complex problems which would be costly or impractical to overcome or control.

The soil scientist placed each mapping unit in the appropriate category for each important land use. Shown in the upper portion of Plate 8 (p. 187) are examples of the categories used, such as flood potential, in which seven categories were needed, and corrosion potential, in which four categories were needed. Even with interpretations such as tree planting, we found that we could use this system. The soils that are suitable for the greatest number of species are represented by green, and the ones with a limited selection by red.

With the statistical charts and the color coding system, the soil scientist and the designer were then able to develop what I call a "Project Capability Interpretation." This is a subjective rating based on the combined judgments of the soil scientist and the designer, and relates only to the project under consideration. For some other land use, or with different design specifications, the ratings of any specific soil series or mapping unit could be, and probably would be, quite different.

Using the site evaluation map and the color coding system a series of fourteen colored interpretive maps depicting the areal

---

*E. E. Offerman, W.U.C., SCS, and E. E. Kubalek, S.S., SCS, Lake Zurich, Illinois, and R. L. Shields, Asst. State S.S., Champaign, Illinois.

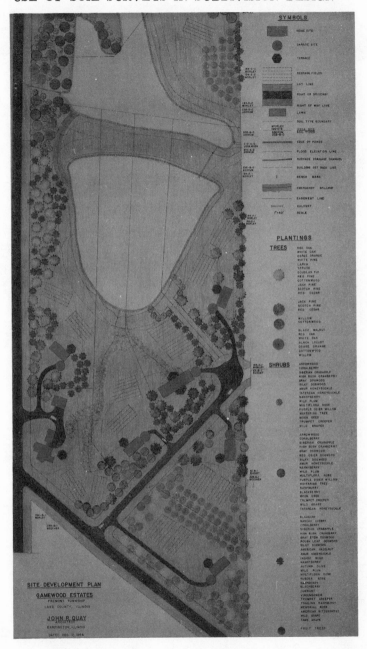

Figure 4. Subdivision plat with 10 building sites.

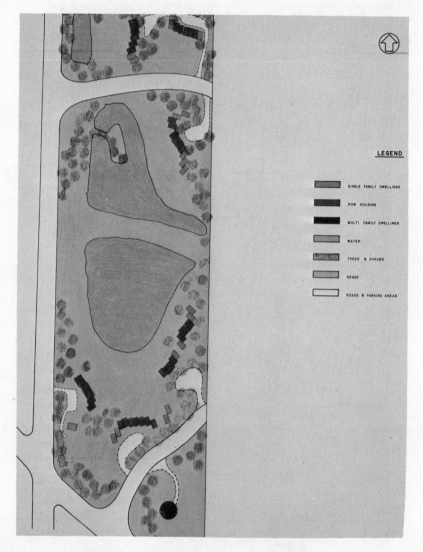

LEGEND

SINGLE FAMILY DWELLINGS

ROW HOUSING

MULTI FAMILY DWELLINGS

WATER

TREES & SHRUBS

GRASS

ROADS & PARKING AREAS

Figure 5.   Sketch plan—high density alternate.

distribution of the individual soil characteristics was derived.
Plates 9 and 10 (p. 188 and 189) are examples of these interpretive maps and show the flood potential and bearing strength interpretations.

After evaluating each of the individual interpretations it was
possible to develop the project capabilities rating and to depict

the areal distribution of the capabilities. (Plate 11, p. 190.) This interpretation indicated that a successful low-density residential subdivision of this area was possible if the designer used caution and designed around some of the major problems.

The next concern was how this subdivision would fit into the surrounding area. As the subdivision was bounded on the south and west by through roads, major interest involved the lands to the east and north of it. Plate 12 (p. 191) shows the soil map of the subdivision and the area to the east and north with a project capabilities interpretation. A study of this map revealed the possibility of future creation of a large lake to the east of the planned subdivision. Topographical data showed that such a lake could be tied into our lakes—a factor to be considered in the subdivision design.

Combining soils data, subdivision, building, health, zoning, and highway regulations, and a little aesthetic judgment, the subdivision plat shown in Figure 4 was developed, giving 10 building sites, each with sufficient useable land for two waste disposal seepage fields and space for patios, garages, orchards, planting screens, etc. Two of the gullies which had been agricultural liabilities, presented ideal opportunities for development as rock gardens in the subdivision plan.

Figure 5 is a preliminary sketch of the parcel showing how this site might be developed when based on a different set of zoning requirements and factors affecting design specifications. In this scheme it has been assumed that central sewers would handle the sanitation problem, thus altering the possible population density of the subdivision. However, the major considerations of site evaluation based on soils data would still apply.

In short, subdivision design based on soils information can minimize a variety of problems which application of a rigid, arbitrary gridiron system of design ignores or accentuates.

<u>LITERATURE CITED</u>

1. American Philosophical Society, 1953. Historic Philadelphia from the Founding Until the Early Nineteenth Century. 330 p. Illustrations and maps.
2. Department of City Planning, City of Chicago, January 1961. Reference Atlas. Ira J. Bach, Commissioner of City Planning. Maps and text.
3. Department of City Planning, City of Chicago, August 1964. Basic Policies for the Comprehensive Plan of Chicago. Ira J. Bach, Commissioner of City Planning. 95 p. Illustrations.
4. Pattison, William D. 1964. Beginnings of the American Rectangular Land Survey System, 1784-1800. Department of Geography, University of Chicago Research Paper #50. 248 p. Illustrations.

5. U.S.D.A. Soil Conservation Service, 1961. Ela Township Soils. 137 p.
   Illustrations.
6. U.S.D.A. Soil Conservation Service, 1963. Lake County Soils. 57 p.
   Illustrations.
7. Village of Barrington, Illinois, Planning Commission, 1958. Comprehensive Plan for the Village of Barrington, Illinois. Evert Kincaid
   and Associates Planning Consultants. Text and maps.
8. Lake County Soil and Water Conservation District. Farm Conservation
   Plan #41, 5-16-58 (Not Published). Text and maps.

CHAPTER 9

THE USE OF AGRICULTURAL SOIL SURVEYS IN THE PLANNING AND CONSTRUCTION OF HIGHWAYS

Thomas H. Thornburn[1]

THE FORTY-EIGHT replies to a recent questionnaire survey of the highway departments of the 50 states indicate that some form of economic analysis is utilized 98% of the time in alternate route location studies, 70% of the time in alternate pavement materials design studies, and 88% of the time in alternate drainage design studies.[1] These are the studies in which soil information may be of considerable value to the engineer, but it seems probable that such information is rarely utilized to great advantage. Before examining the kind of information which soil surveys may contribute to the solution of the total highway planning and design problem it is advantageous to obtain a perspective on the possible magnitude of the contribution.

The first step in the planning for a given highway route is a high-level decision making process required to designate the areas to be served. Thus, certain corridors or bands of interest are identified as possible connections between two widely separated points, such as Chicago, Illinois, and New Orleans, Louisiana. Narrower bands of interest would then be considered for a segment of this route in Illinois, for example between Chicago and the southern tip of the state, at Cairo, than would be the case for the whole route. High-level decisions might still be required to identify a few important Illinois communities which should be served, but once these are established successively lower level decisions are required (1) to plan specific projects, (2) to designate appropriate individual highway links within the bands of interest, (3) to select the most desirable link and to formulate the preliminary engineering design and (4) to prepare the final design plans and specifications. While terrain information will generally play little or no part in making the decisions at the highest level it becomes increasingly important in carrying out the engineering work required in the four lower level decisions.

1. Department of Civil Engineering, University of Illinois, Urbana, Ill.

In the last few years highway departments have given increasing attention to the economics of highway location and design. In 1959 a workshop conference on this subject was sponsored by the Highway Research Board.[2] In reviewing the record of this conference, it is discouraging to a soils engineer to note how many factors, such as expected traffic, changes in land use, and highway user benefits, seem to be more important economic considerations than the cost of engineering and construction. It is quite apparent, however, that some type of systems analysis is being or will soon be applied to all major highway improvements in order to justify them or to rank them in order of relative need. Furthermore, it appears that systems analysis will soon be employed for decision making in all phases of the highway program down to the final design phase. A major reason for this is the adaptability of computer techniques to such analyses.

The Civil Engineering Systems Laboratory at Massachusetts Institute of Technology has already prepared computer programs to evaluate most of the highway construction variables.[3,4] Even though the use of such programs is in the elementary stages for many aspects of the design and location problem, most highway departments are already using computers to plot profiles, set grade stakes, and compute earthwork quantities.

The breakdown of total annual cost of a particular highway alignment (link) can be formulated as in equation 1. The asterisk indicates that the annual capital cost is the only factor which would be significantly affected by variations in soil conditions. However, the annual maintenance cost will also be affected unless the pavement design is appropriate for the existing soils.

$$TAC = ACC* + AUC + AMC \tag{1}$$

where TAC = Total Annual Cost ($)
ACC = Annual Capital Cost ($)
AUC = Annual User Cost ($)
AMC = Annual Maintenance Cost ($)

The annual capital cost is a function of the total construction cost and the capital recovery factor as shown in equation 2. This factor can be computed from the interest rate assumed and the expected service life of the pavement. The choice of these two items becomes particularly important in benefit-cost analysis but has little influence when comparing alternate alignments.

$$ACC = (tcc) \times (CRF) \tag{2}$$

tcc* = total construction cost
CRF = Capital Recovery Factor

where   CRF depends on
  i = interest rate per interest period (%)
  n = service life (years) (normally 20)

The total construction cost is the sum of various costs shown in equation 3. Again the asterisks indicate those items which are influenced by local soil conditions, however it may often be difficult to evaluate the effect of different types of soils on the magnitude of all cost factors which are so influenced. The physical data from agricultural soil maps and soil-engineering interpretations should be useful, at least, in making estimates of earthwork, pavement, and right-of-way costs. To be strictly correct the total construction cost should be reduced by a factor based on the salvage value of the right-of-way, but it is so difficult to estimate a reasonable salvage factor that in most analyses it is assumed to be zero.

$$tcc = ec* + sc* + pc* + dc* + ic + rc* + lc* \qquad (3)$$

where   ec = earthwork cost ($)
  sc = structures cost ($)
  pc = pavement cost ($)
  dc = drainage cost ($)
  ic = interchange cost ($)
  rc = relocation cost ($)
  lc = land and right-of-way cost ($)

(Salvage values assumed to be zero.)

In the MIT analysis, and probably in most other analyses used by highway departments, the earthwork cost is computed primarily from the relationship between the selected grade line and the original terrain. Such an analysis yields data on the amount of earth which must be moved from cut sections or borrow areas and placed in fill sections. Seldom is any consideration given to the differences in the cost of excavating and placing different types of materials. Presumably it costs as much to excavate, move, and recompact a well-graded sand as it does a highly plastic clay. Unfortunately, there is little published information on the relative cost of earthwork in various types of materials. Until it can be shown that soil characteristics do have a significant influence on earthwork costs there is slight chance that it will be taken into consideration in making cost estimates.

The structures cost is dependent upon foundation conditions, but unfortunately this can seldom be taken into consideration in

making the preliminary cost estimates. While soil surveys could
be helpful in estimating this item, generally the depth of structural foundations is such that only detailed site investigations can
provide the necessary data to make a reliable estimate of foundation type and cost.

Pavement cost should certainly be related to the subgrade
conditions, since nearly all methods of pavement design include a
factor which is related to the subgrade soil classification. Nevertheless, it is common practice to prepare a standard pavement
cross-section which is presumably suitable for all alignments
under consideration. Usually, no allowance is made for design
revisions where the soil conditions are exceptionally good or exceptionally poor, at least not in making preliminary estimates.
In most cases, however, the standard design is selected at least
in part on the basis of local experience which includes considerations of general soil conditions and not for individual kinds of
soils.

Although drainage cost is partly dependent upon general soil
conditions, which influence the amount of runoff, the major part
of this cost is connected with the design and construction of
drains, inlets, ditches, collector systems and culverts. Thus, the
overall cost is influenced only in a minor way by the permeability
of the soils in the various drainage areas and probably is not
worthy of consideration until the final design stage.

Interchange cost is primarily dependent upon the number of
interchanges to be built and would generally be influenced by soil
conditions only to the extent that extra earthwork and right-of-way
would be involved.

Under relocation cost, consideration may be given to special
items of cost such as relocation of drainage ways or the filling
of ponded areas. Again, in most analyses the quantities of excavation and borrow are the prime items for consideration.
Under this heading, however, computations for excavating and
filling of peat bogs could be considered. Here a knowledge of
the location, kind, and amount of soils having low bearing qualities would be of definite value to the engineer and could result
in a considerable savings of one alignment over another.

Land and right-of-way cost is obviously related to the kinds
of local soils, at least in rural areas, with the present and prospective land use having an important bearing on the cost. Any
reasonable system of evaluating these costs must certainly be
related to the soil and land use factor. Within a given corridor,
however, the cost differential between alternate lines of right-of-
way is often insignificant.

An approximate breakdown of construction costs for a 7-mile rural segment of an interstate highway in Massachusetts which was tested by the MIT group gave the following percentages: earthwork, 43%; pavement, 27%; structures, 20%; right-of-way, 8%; and drainage, 2%. These costs amounted to about 10% of Total Annual Cost; the Annual User Cost amounted to about 90%. Note that the earthwork and pavement cost together amount to 70% of the total construction cost. Although these percentages are not directly applicable to other highway construction projects it is probable that the first three items will always represent a major part of the construction costs in rural areas. Local soil conditions directly influence the costs of each of these items, and should be taken into consideration.

The complete analysis shows that the annual construction cost amounts to only about 10% of the total annual cost. Thus, in the final economic analysis items of annual user cost such as fuel cost, tire cost, vehicle maintenance and depreciation, traffic volumes, and user time, become vastly more important than construction costs. Although the evaluation of user costs is surely as uncertain as the computations for construction costs, user costs may be the controlling factors in the choice of alignments. Thus, the engineer may often lose his battle to reduce construction costs through the choice of a more favorable alignment from the engineering standpoint. This, however, does not relieve him of the responsibility of providing the transportation hierarchy with valid estimates on which to base an economic decision. The character of the soils should be taken into consideration in providing these estimates and the information that can be obtained from agricultural soil maps and their interpretations can and should be utilized in several phases of the construction cost analysis.

In the preliminary evaluation of alternate highway alignments general soil maps, such as soil association maps, are more useful than detailed soil maps. Their utility stems from the fact that generalized soil maps show the location and amount of the different kinds of soil over broad areas. The soil map units also give information directly related to the soil parent materials. These materials usually form the subgrade for high-type highway facilities. The following example illustrates how available soil survey data could be used in an interstate highway location problem in Illinois.

Figure 1 is a portion of a soil map for Ford County, Illinois.[5] Superimposed upon the soil map are two possible alignments for a ten-mile segment of a north-south interstate highway.

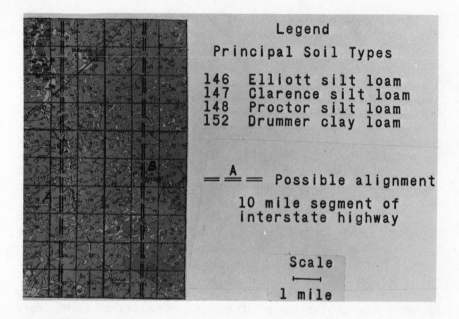

Figure 1. Portion of soil survey map, Ford County, Illinois (1933),
showing alternate highway alignments. University of Illinois Agr. Exp. Sta.

These alignments are three miles apart and lie only a few miles
west of U.S. Route 45 which forms a major portion of the present
main highway route between Chicago and Cairo. Thus, both alignments could be considered to be within the band of interest for
an interstate route connecting these cities. Proposed Route A
lies primarily within an area designated as soil type 146, Elliott
silt loam, whereas Route B lies mostly within soil type 147,
Clarence silt loam. Minor amounts of soil type 152, Drummer
clay loam, are shown along both routes.

Figure 2 shows the results of a reevaluation of the area
under consideration on the basis of field work accomplished in
the 1950's.[6] It can be seen that Route A lies primarily in an
area underlain by parent material 4, silty clay loam till, with a
minor amount of parent material 3, loam till. Route B lies in
an area underlain mostly by parent material 5, silty clay drift,
and parent material 6, clay drift with some parent material 4.
For the purpose of the analysis it is assumed that Route A lies
entirely in parent material 4 and Route B lies entirely in parent
materials 5 and 6. Pertinent physical characteristics of the four
different types of glacial drift found in the area are shown in

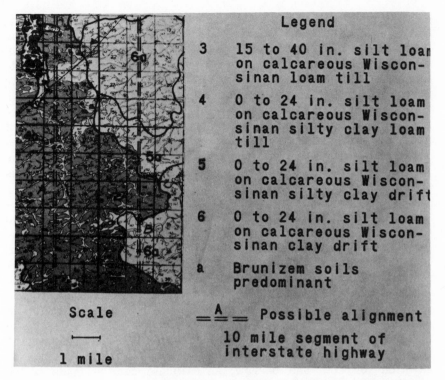

Legend

3 15 to 40 in. silt loan on calcareous Wisconsinan loam till

4 0 to 24 in. silt loam on calcareous Wisconsinan silty clay loam till

5 0 to 24 in. silt loam on calcareous Wisconsinan silty clay drift

6 0 to 24 in. silt loam on calcareous Wisconsinan clay drift

a Brunizem soils predominant

Scale

1 mile

=A= Possible alignment

10 mile segment of interstate highway

Figure 2. Portion of unpublished soil association map, Ford County, Illinois, showing alternate highway alignments. Agronomy Department, University of Illinois, Agr. Exp. Sta.

Table 1 as taken from a recent agricultural publication. [7] It is apparent that significant differences exist among the four different parent materials and that these differences should certainly be reflected in their engineering behavior. In the AASHO system of engineering classification of soils, parent material 3 classifies as A-4, parent material 4 as A-6, and parent materials 5 and 6 as A-7-6. [8] The increase in the numerical classification indicates successively poorer materials for subgrades.

Table 1. Typical properties of glacial drift.

Type of drift	Sand and gravel	Silt	Clay	Liquid limit	Plasticity index	AASHO class
Loam till	31	46	23	26	9	A-4
Silty clay loam till	16	53	31	35	16	A-6
Silty clay drift	13	47	40	41	22	A-7-6
Clay drift	6	39	55	48	26	A-7-6

Because of their high clay contents parent materials 4, 5, and 6 usually exist at natural water contents above the optimum required for proper compaction. Meager data indicate that parent material 4 often exists at natural water contents 5% above optimum and that it is not unusual for parent materials 5 and 6 to occur at natural water contents 10% above optimum. Although highway engineers recognize the difficulties of properly compacting soils which have natural water contents several per cent above optimum, such difficulties are seldom anticipated during the construction planning phases. This is largely the result of the lack of accumulated data on the natural water content of various types of soils.

Recent conversations with a major Illinois highway contracting firm reveal that their bids for earthwork would be influenced considerably by the nature of the soil and its natural water content. As the water content of the soil increases above optimum, it becomes more difficult to excavate the soil with ordinary earthmoving equipment. At water contents as high as 10% over optimum it would probably be necessary to excavate with draglines rather than scrapers. Furthermore, the rate of excavation is controlled by the rate at which the soil dries back to optimum and can be compacted in the fill sections. Assuming an earthwork requirement of 350,000 cubic yards per mile, including excavation for cuts and borrow, an estimate can be made of the relative costs of construction in the two different soil areas as shown in Table 2. The estimated unit price of earthwork for each alternate is based on reasonable contractor costs in Illinois at the present time.

Table 2.   Comparison of earthwork costs.   Ten-mile segment
of interstate highway.

Route designation	A	B
Soil parent material area	4	5 and 6
AASHO classification	A-6	A-7-6
Natural water content, estimated amount above optimum	5%	10%
Estimated earthwork unit price per cu. yd.	$0.50	$0.68
Total estimated earthwork cost, 10 mile section*	$1,750,000	$2,380,000
Cost differential - earthwork	---	$ 630,000
Percent cost differential - earthwork	---	36%

The differences in the two soil areas also result in the different requirements for pavement design shown in Table 3. The pavement thicknesses are based on the present bituminous pavement design policy of the Illinois Division of Highways. [9]

Table 3. Comparison of bituminous pavement design costs.

Route designation	A	B
Soil parent material area	4	5 and 6
AASHO classification	A-6	A-7-6
Estimated California bearing ratio (CRB)	3	2
Estimated structural number*	4. 75	5. 25
Design thickness, surface, in.	4	4
stabilized base course, in.	8	10
subbase course, in.	12	11. 5
Excess base course required, cu. yd.	--	18,750
Cost differential, pavement	--	$180,000

* Based on 20-year expected life, 20,000 vehicles per day, 95% passenger cars, 2-1/2% small trucks, 2-1/2% multiple units.

The CBR value expresses the strength of the subgrade soil after saturation. Even though there is very little difference between the two values there is enough to make a difference in the required pavement thickness. The structural number is estimated on the basis of the CBR value, an assumed life expectancy of 20 years and certain assumptions as to the amount and type of traffic. The traffic rate is a reasonable prediction for such a facility in 1975 and the traffic type distribution is that suggested for the MIT analysis by the Massachusetts Department of Highways. The design thickness for each layer of the pavement represents the minimum thickness allowable for the particular structural number. While it would be possible to change the design by increasing the thicknesses of either the surface or base course layer, this would almost certainly result in increased costs. It will be noted that the principal difference between the two designs is in the thickness of base course required. Although Route B requires 0.5 inch less of subbase than Route A, the specifications for the poorer soil require that the subbase be a higher quality material. Therefore, for the purposes of this analysis is the costs of the subbase for the two routes are assumed equal.

An estimate of the increase in total construction of the highway primarily in parent material areas 5 and 6 (Route B) is given in Table 4. Based on the estimated cost of construction of the same facility in parent material area 4 (Route A) the increase amounts to 18.5%. This is certainly a significant cost item. Even if it is in error by a factor of two, the cost of ignoring the implications of the soil conditions cannot be easily justified.

The preceding discussion has emphasized the importance of using agricultural soil survey information during the preliminary planning of new highway alignments for it is felt that the greatest savings can be realized at this new time. It has shown that not

Table 4.   Comparison of total segment of interstate highway.

Estimated earthwork cost for Route A, area of parent material 4	$1,750,000
Estimated total construction cost, Route A*	4,375,000
Estimated increase in earthwork cost for Route B, area of parent materials 5 and 6	630,000
Estimated increase in bituminous pavement cost for Route B	180,000
Estimated increase in total construction cost for Route B	810,000
Estimated percentage increase in total construction cost for Route B over Route A	18.5%

* Assuming earthwork represents 40% of total construction cost.

only detailed soil maps and interpretations in published county soil surveys are of value, but also soil association maps, area soil reports and reports containing correlations between pedologic and engineering classifications.   Modern published agricultural soil surveys contain much of the data which has been utilized.   A random sampling of 21 soil surveys published since November 1959, indicates that on the average actual engineering test data are presented on about 35% of the soil series mapped in a given county.   Variations in the number of series with actual test data range from a minimum of 10% to a maximum of 89%.   Although engineering test data are not usually presented for all soil series in the survey area the modern published soil survey does contain estimates of the physical soil properties for all of the soils. These estimates are made by engineers and soil scientists and are based on test data and other information available.   Sometimes missing information can be found in summary reports such as the special FHA publication.[10]   Often, however, the engineer is lacking critical information on some series.   Nevertheless, he will usually find enough data to help him to estimate the physical properties of the parent material.

Even without complete engineering test data however, the soil surveys are extremely useful in detailed location planning.   One obvious use is to determine the location of organic soils and other soils with low bearing capacity.   Table 5 gives the computations for the cost of excavating and backfilling a peat bog 1000 feet long, and having an average depth of 10 feet on the usual 300-foot right-of-way for an interstate highway.   Again, the estimated unit costs of excavation, disposal and granular backfill are believed to be representative of costs in parts of Illinois at the present time.   If only one such peat deposit were encountered in a 10-mile section of interstate highway it could easily increase the cost of the section by nearly $200,000 which amounts to 4.5% of the typical total construction costs estimated for Route A in Table 4.

Table 5. Cost of peat excavation and replacement for deposit
1000 feet long, average depth of 10 feet on 300-foot
right-of-way, approximately 111,000 cubic yards

Estimated cost of excavation, per cu. yd	$ 0.40
Estimated cost of disposal, per cu. yd.	0.55
Estimated cost of granular backfill, per cu. yd.	0.80
Total, per cu. yd.	1.75
Total estimated cost of excavation and backfill 1.75 × 111,000	194,250.00
Estimated total construction cost of 10 mile segment of interstate highway (no peat)	$4,375,000.00
Increased cost of 10 mile section	4.4%

Similar computations could be made for alignments where
rock lies close to the surface by estimating the cost of rock excavation for an average depth of rock cut. Soil surveys provide
enough information on the depth to shallow rock to make valid
preliminary estimates. Since the cost of rock excavation is
usually three to four times that of common earth excavation, the
cost of an alignment over shallow rock might easily be 50 to
100% greater than one where only earth excavation was required.
    A recent study made by the New York State Department of
Public Works [11] helps to provide additional information on the
relative cost of earthwork in various types of terrain. In this
study the soils and geologic conditions of the terrain traversed
by two alternate routes were first identified, delineated and classified. Each alternate was considered as a possible location for a
90-mile section of interstate highway in eastern New York state.
The reconnaissance was carried out by a team composed of a
soils engineer, an engineering geologist and a soil scientist in
approximately three weeks. Five published agricultural soil surveys and six geologic reports were utilized in the reconnaissance.
The actual earthwork costs of similar class highways constructed
in the past on similar terrains were studied, and relative earthwork cost factors per mile were assigned to each class of terrain
involved in the proposed routes. Table 6 shows the earthwork
factors used for each class of terrain and the relative earthwork
cost for the two routes. The earthwork factors are particularly
interesting since they are not estimates, but are based on actual
construction bid costs. The cost of construction in granular outwash is an especially appropriate basis for comparison since this
type of terrain is usually nearly level and the materials in the
deposit are easily excavated and compacted under most climatic
situations. On the basis of this study it was concluded that earthwork costs for a lowland (Champlain) route would actually be

Table 6. Relative earthwork costs, New York interstate highway—
92-mile section.

Terrain class and type		Earthwork Factor, F	Adirondack Route, M×F*	Champlain Route, M×F
1	Granular outwash	1.0	27.5	1.0
2	Glacial til	1.7	13.8	-
3	Rough rock lands	4.3	195.2	106.2
3X	Class 3, restricted	6.7	-	24.1
4A	Lacustrine sediments	1.5	-	55.2
4B	Marine sediments	3.5	-	56.4
4C	Sand over 4A	1.0	9.1	7.3
5	Major swamps	7.7	7.7	20.8
	Total		253.3	271.0

* M× F = Mileage × Earthwork Factor

about 7% greater than those for a mountainous (Adirondack) route. In addition, it was estimated, on the basis of land use, that more than 50% of the lowland route would traverse land having a value of from 10 to 20 times the value of the lands traversed by the mountainous route. Although this was not taken into consideration in the earthwork cost analysis, it would certainly enter into economic considerations of final route selection.

One of the most important uses of soil survey information is in conjunction with the final detailed engineering soil survey. [12] There can be no doubt that a modern soil map published to the scale of 1:20,000 is an invaluable aid in planning and conducting a satisfactory engineering soil survey for design purposes. Furthermore, it will provide information on areas outside of the right-of-way line which should be explored as possible sources of granular materials. Byers has stated "Although claims that the use of these (pedologic) maps will result in less field sampling or less laboratory testing would be hard to either prove or disprove, it is unquestionable that they do make possible a more intelligent interpretation of such data as are obtained. This in turn provides a better basis for highway design and construction resulting in more economic highway transportation." [13]

The value of the agricultural soil survey is greatly enhanced if engineering test data on several profiles of each series are given for then the soil engineer can concentrate his soil borings in the most variable area. Recent work in Illinois has indicated that some soil series are inherently quite variable in their engineering properties while others are surprisingly uniform. A comparison of some statistics for two Humic-Gley soils with similar physical properties is given in Table 7. [14] The data show that the degree of variability in the A horizon is similar

Table 7. Variability of soil types.

		Statistical data*					
		Sable SCL			Drummer SCL		
		Mean	S	CV	Mean	S	CV
Horizon and property							
A	Liquid limit	52	7	14	50	8	15
	Plasticity index	24	5	22	24	6	23
	Percent clay (−0. 002 mm)	34	4	13	33	5	17
B	Liquid limit	50	4	9	45	8	18
	Plasticity index	27	4	15	25	6	26
	Percent clay (−0. 002 mm)	36	4	10	34	7	20
C	Liquid limit	42	7	16	36	9	26
	Plasticity index	22	7	33	18	9	47
	Percent clay (−0. 002 mm)	31	6	20	27	9	35

* Mean, standard deviation and coefficient of variation based on 15 samples from Cass, Henderson and Livingston counties for Sable and 15 samples from Livingston, Menard and Will counties for Drummer.

for the two soils, but that the B and C horizons of Drummer silty clay loam are considerably more variable than those of the Sable silty clay loam. Based upon data of this type a sampling program can be designed which will reduce the number of borings made in a relatively uniform soil type and increase the number made in a variable soil type. A recent study of such an experimentally de-signed soil survey for a $3\frac{1}{2}$ mile section of right-of-way in Will County, indicated that the number of borings in a variable soil series, such as Drummer, should be increased more than 50% as compared to the number which would be made in it at regular spacing of 150 feet.[15] The number of borings in the more uni-form soils would of course be reduced accordingly.

The utilization of agricultural soil surveys in the design of high type pavements has already been mentioned, but they are equally useful in the design of low-cost pavements for secondary roads. Although the correlation between pavement design parame-ters and soil series is not perfect, in many instances the engi-neering data contained in the soil report is sufficient for design when amplified by only a small amount of laboratory testing of samples.[16,17] In Washington state the thickness requirements for various types of highways have been determined for various counties on the basis of soil associations with modifications for variations in rainfall and frost penetration.[18] Such a design procedure depends on the accumulation of a great amount of engi-neering and performance data used in conjunction with modern agricultural soil maps and reports.

The data contained in modern detailed soil surveys have an obvious application to the problem of improving subgrades by stabilization procedures. Data on the physical properties of the various soils found within the proposed right-of-way indicate those areas which are underlain by poor subgrade materials, and also provide a basis for choosing appropriate stabilizing agents. Correlations between chemical stabilizer requirements and soil series seem to be particularly good. Work carried on by the Portland Cement Association has indicated that, "—cement factors can be established for each horizon of a given soil series and no further soil-cement tests are then needed on future work involving the same series." [19] Even where such correlations do not exist published data on the grain-size characteristics of sandy soils may enable the engineer to greatly reduce the amount of laboratory testing required to determine the correct cement factor. [20] Once the amount of stabilizing additive is chosen, reliable estimates of the cost of the improvement can be made.

Recent work at the University of Illinois has shown that a soils reactivity with lime for lime-soil stabilization is determined by natural soil properties. [21]   Thus, there is a good correlation between lime-reactivity and soil series. Furthermore, the applicability of lime stabilization to a given soil area can usually be predicted on the basis of physical and especially chemical data contained in published agricultural soil reports. A few important conclusions of this investigation which verifies the use of pedologic data in predicting the lime-reactivity of Illinois soils are as follows:

1. Organic carbon greatly retards lime-soil reactions, therefore the A horizons of most soils do not react satisfactorily,
2. High soil pH is indicative of good reactivity, therefore
   a. solonetzic soils are very lime-reactive,
   b. C horizons of most soils react satisfactorily,
3. Poorly drained soils display higher lime-reactivities than well-drained soils.

Finally, the uses of agricultural soil surveys during the construction phase should be mentioned. Although only modern published soil surveys have interpretive tables which contain valuable qualitative information for engineers, with relatively little knowledge of pedologic classification the engineer or contractor can make his own interpretations from soil profile descriptions in older reports. A knowledge of the position of the ground water table in the spring of the year can prevent much wasted time and effort on the part of the contractor. As an example, the specifications for the Northern Illinois Toll Road required the removal of organic topsoil under low fills. It happened that the spring of the first major construction season was one of high rainfall, but because of time limitations the contractors were eager to begin work in early May. It was soon evident, however, that topsoil stripping of the Humic-Gley soils to the necessary depths of 12 inches or more could not be accomplished at this time. Because of the high water table and the character of the soils, heavy excavating equipment could not operate. Nevertheless, almost every contractor persisted in his attempts to perform this operation until he had consumed many hours of operator and equipment time by repeatedly miring his equipment in the soft soil and then extricating it. A meager knowledge of soil engineering problems and the proper use of agricultural soil surveys would have eliminated these wasted efforts. By the middle of June the water tables had dropped and the operation could be carried on without particular difficulty. Similarly, much wasted effort and poor construction can be avoided by knowing which soils can be satisfactorily graded during the winter season without the danger of leaving soft pockets in the subgrade during the spring thaw. The engineering section of modern soil reports commonly classifies the various soil series in this respect.

Many other examples could be given, which show how soil maps and their interpretations can help to delineate construction problems. Table 8 lists the various kinds of engineering

Table 8. Engineering interpretations contained in modern
agricultural soil reports

Engineering classification	
Textural classification	
Reaction	
General suitability for	subgrade
	source of topsoil
	source of sand and gravel
	source of common borrow
	foundations for embankments
	winter grading
Soil-water relations	seasonal high water table
	drainage class
	permeability
	shrink-swell potential
	erosion hazard
Special problems	seepage in cuts
	stability of slopes
	alignment of highway
	frost susceptibility
	flooding
	cemented or compacted layers
	wind erosion
	shallow bedrock

information found in modern soil survey, however a single report may not contain all these interpretations. Unfortunately, too few soil engineers and highway contractors are aware of the utility or availability of this information.

The natural system of soil classification used in agricultural soil surveys forms an ideal basis for the study of pavement performance which in turn controls design. The Michigan State Highway Department has made full use of this system.[22] The failure of most other highway departments to make the best use of this classification results, at least in part, from the lack of personnel trained in the interpretation of pedologic data. Modern agricultural soil survey reports containing sections with engineering interpretations help to remedy this situation. There remains only the problems of making many more of these reports available as rapidly as possible and of persuading highway engineers to use the information which they contain to the best advantage.

LITERATURE CITED

1. Glancy, D. M. Utilization of economic analysis by state highway departments. Highway Research Board Highway Research Record 77. pp. 121-132, 1965.
2. Economic analysis in highway programming, location and design: Workshop conference proceedings. Highway Research Board Special Report 56, 1960.
3. Roberts, P. O., Jr., and J. H. Suhrbier. Link analysis for route location. Highway Research Board Highway Research Record 77, pp. 19-47, 1965.
4. Roberts, P. O., and J. H. Suhrbier. Highway location analysis, an example problem. Massachusetts Inst. Tech. Dept. Civil Eng. Res. Report R62-40, 1962.
5. Smith, R. S., H. Wascher, and G. D. Smith. Ford County Soils. University of Illinois, Agr. Exp. Sta. Soil Report 54, Rev., 1941.
6. Map of soil association areas of Ford County. University of Illinois Agr. Exp. Sta.
7. Wascher, H. L., et al. Characteristics of soils associated with glacial tills in northeastern Illinois. University of Illinois Agr. Exp. Sta. Bull. 665, 1960.
8. Standard specifications for highway materials, 8th Ed. Amer. Assn. State Highway Officials, 1961.
9. Manual for the structural design of bituminous pavements in Illinois. Illinois Division of Highways, 1965.
10. Engineering soil classification for residential developments. Federal Housing Administration No. 373, Rev., 1961.
11. Hofmann, W. P., and J. B. Flecktenstein. Comparison of general routes by terrain appraisal methods in New York State. Highway Research Board Proc., Vol. 39, pp. 640-649, 1960.

12. Felt, E. J. Soil series names as a basis for interpretive soil classification for engineering purposes. Symposium on the Identification
and Classification of Soils, Amer. Soc. Testing and Materials Spec.
Tech. Publ. No. 113, pp. 62-84, 1951.
13. Byers, M. E. Use of pedologic map in a highway soilssurvey. Soil
Mapping: Methods and Applications. Highway Research Board Bull.
299, pp. 9-18, 1961.
14. Liu, T. K., and T. H. Thornburn. Engineering index properties of
some surficial soils in Illinois. University of Illinois Eng. Exp. Sta.
Bull. 477, 1965.
15. Liu, T. K., and T. H. Thornburn. Statistically controlled engineering
soil survey. University of Illinois Civil Eng. Studies, Soil Mechanics
Series No. 9, 1965.
16. Hicks, L. D. Use of soil survey data in design of highways. Engineering Applications of Soil Surveying and Mapping. Highway Research
Board Bull. 83, pp. 32-39, 1953.
17. Evans, F. K. Use of soil maps in operation and planning of county
highway activities. Air Photo and Soil Mapping Methods: Appraisal
and Application, Highway Research Board Bull. 180, pp. 33-38, 1958.
18. Ekse, M. The value of soil test data in local and regional road planning. Symposium on Application of Soil Testing in Highway Design
and Construction, Amer. Soc. Testing and Materials, Spec. Tech.
Publ. No. 239, pp. 74-88, 1959.
19. Leadabrand, J. A., L. T. Norling, and A. C. Hurless. Soil series as
a basis for determining cement requirements for soil-cement construction. Soil Series Cement Requirements. Highway Research Board
Bull. 148, pp. 1-17, 1957.
20. Short-cut test procedures for sandy soils. Soil-Cement Laboratory
Handbook, Portland Cement Association, 1959.
21. Thompson, M. R., Lime-reactivity of Illinois soils as it relates to
compressive strength, Ph.D. dissertation submitted to the Graduate
College of the University of Illinois, 1964. University Microfilms
No. 65-3683.
22. Field Manual of Soil Engineering, 4th Ed., Michigan State Highway
Department, 1960.

CHAPTER 10

USE OF SOIL SURVEYS IN PLANNING FOR RECREATION

P. H. Montgomery and Frank C. Edminster[1]

THE DEMAND FOR outdoor recreation is growing rapidly and more and more of America's farm and ranch land is being used by the public for recreation. Most rural land accessible to users can be converted to some form of recreational use. There are many considerations, physical and economic, that determine the potential of an area for outdoor recreation. The kind of soil dictates to a large degree the type and location of recreational facilities. Some soils are not desirable sites for campsites, play areas, picnic grounds, cabin sites, or natural study areas; other soils are very desirable sites for recreational use. Knowledge of the soils of an area—a farm, ranch, community, watershed, or county—provide fundamental information needed in recreation planning.

Soil surveys provide for classifying, defining, and delineating each kind of soil and making predictions of soil behavior under specific management. Soil surveys are made and published for designated areas such as counties, projects, or soil conservation districts. The soils within the area are mapped and classified without regard for existing or expected land ownership boundaries or types of use. Each delineated soil is defined so that the information is available for planning different kinds of land use.

Each kind of soil has its peculiar set of characteristics and qualities which are described in terms that can be observed. These include soil texture; color; structure; consistence; depth (to rock, hardpan, water table, etc.); kind and amount of coarse fragments; kind, thickness, and sequence of soil layers; organic matter content; reaction; and slope. When accurately defined a specific soil can be distinguished from all other kinds of soil.

In the survey area soil units are recognized, defined, and delineated on aerial photo maps to show the location, size and slope of the soil areas. The mapping is done at different degrees of intensity depending upon the uses to be made of it. On high- and medium-intensity soil surveys, phases of soil series are the common map unit. These map units are classified, named, and correlated within the

---

1. Assistant Director, Soil Survey Interpretations, and Soil Conservationist (Recreation), Soil Conservation Service, USDA.

National system of soil classification.[1,2] Low-intensity, or reconnaissance, surveys have limited value for recreational planning.

The same soil properties that affect agricultural uses of soil
are the ones that affect their use for recreation. The interpretations are different but they go back to the same basic principles of
water movement, shrink-swell potential, fertilizer use efficiency,
susceptibility to erosion, and others. Our first job is to know the
kind of soil, then make the interpretations for the intended use.
Thus modern soil maps are a basic tool for recreational planning as
well as for other purposes.

All soils can be used for recreational activities of some kind.
Some have no soil limitations for specific kinds of recreational use;
others have moderate to severe limitations for certain uses. In
fact, some kinds of soil are dangerous if used for certain recreational activities, such as camping. The use of soils subject to flash
flooding or landslides can lead to loss of life and property.

The effects of a given soil property often vary with different
uses. The following are some of the soil properties that singly or
in combination with others commonly affect recreational uses of
soils.

Soils subject to flooding have severe limitations for use as
sites for camps and recreation buildings. If soils subject to flooding are not protected by dikes, levees, or other flood prevention
structures they should not be developed for campsites or vacation
cottages. These soils are better suited for hiking or nature study
areas, or for greenbelt open space, if the flooding is not too frequent.

-    Soils that are wet all year, even if not flooded, have severe soil
limitations for campsites, recreational roads and trails, playgrounds, and picnic areas. Soils that are wet only part of the year
or those that have a water table that moves up and down without
reaching the surface are not easily detected by most people. These
soils have severe limitations for most recreational uses. Soils that
dry out slowly after rains present problems where intensive use is
contemplated.

Droughty soils also have limitations for many recreational
uses. On such sites, grass cover needed for playing fields is difficult to establish and maintain. Access roads may be excessively
dusty. Vehicles are easily mired down in sandy soils and soil blow-
ing is common. Knowledge of these soil problems enables planners
to use corrective conservation practices, such as irrigation, or to
choose alternative locations.

The ability of a soil to support a load is important in many
kinds of recreational activities. Some soils when wet fail to support
structures such as access roads, trails, and buildings.

Slope affects the use of soils for recreation. Nearly level, well drained, permeable, stone-free soils have few or no limitations for use as playgrounds, campsites, sites for recreational buildings, roads, and trails. Soils with steep slopes often have severe limitations for most recreational uses. On the other hand, steeply sloping soils are essential for ski runs and are desirable for hiking areas, scenic values, and vacation cottage sites "with a view." Of course, deep, gently sloping, and moderately sloping soils can be leveled for campsites, playgrounds, and building sites where the cost is justified. Where this is done it is especially urgent that effective soil conservation practices be applied and maintained based on the specific conditions.

Soil depth affects many uses. Soils underlain by bedrock to shallow depths cannot be leveled for playgrounds and campsites except at high cost. Roads, trails, and basements are very difficult to construct on these soils. It is difficult to establish vegetation on soils shallow to impervious soil layers or rock thus making them poor locations for playing fields and other intensive use areas.

Surface texture is an important soil property to consider. High sand or clay content in the surface soils is undesirable for playgrounds, campsites, or other uses that involve heavy foot traffic by people or horses. Soils high in clay become sticky when wet and do not dry out quickly after rains. On the other hand, loose sandy soils are undesirable as they are unstable when dry. Sandy loam and loam surface texteured soils that also have other favorable characteristics are the most desirable for recreational uses involving heavy use by people.

The presence of stones, rocks, cobbles, or gravel limits the use of some soils for recreational uses. Very stony, stony, rocky, or gravelly soils have severe to moderate limitations for use as campsites and playgrounds. In some instances it is feasible to remove the stones, thus eliminating the hazard. Rounded gravels and stones present hazards on steeply sloping soils used for foot trails.

Sanitary facilities are essential for most modern recreational areas and septic tanks are often the only means of waste disposal. Some soils absorb septic tank effluent rapidly and other soils absorb it very slowly. Soils that are slowly permeable, poorly drained, shallow to rock, subject to flooding, or steeply sloping all have severe limitations for septic tank filter fields.[3] In some cases where soils cannot handle the volume of waste involved, sewage lagoons can be used. These also are feasible only in soils that meet the special requirements for sewage lagoons.

Productive capacity of soils for vegetation of different kinds is closely related to the feasibility of many recreation enterprises.

The ability of soils to grow sods that can take concentrated human traffic has already been noted as a factor in such areas as playgrounds and campsites. The development of such vegetative conservation practices as shade tree plantings, living fences, plant screens, and barriers to trespass is guided by soil conditions. The capacity of an area to produce economically harvestable crops of game is dependent, in part, on the productive ability of its soils.[4]

The suitability of the soil for impounding water reflects, in considerable measure, the kind of soil at the impoundment site as well as in the watershed above the impoundment. Fertile soils, or soils capable of effective use of artificial fertilizers, generally make fertile waters. And fertile waters produce good fish crops which, with good management, produce good fishing. On the other hand, extremely acid soils associated with a proposed water impoundment may be a critical limitation to the development of good fishing.

Thus we find that basic soil qualities and characteristics are closely associated with the various types of outdoor recreation activities. By knowing the characteristics and qualities of the different kinds of soils and their behavior, and with the aid of a soil map soil scientists and other specialists can develop soil interpretations for recreational uses. Interpretations for recreational uses can best be made locally by those familiar with the soils and conditions in the area. Soils in an area are normally grouped into three or five groups according to their limitations for a specific recreational use.

1. None to slight soil limitations—Soils relatively free of limitations that affect the intended use or the limitations are easy to overcome.

2. Moderate soil limitations—Soils with moderate limitations resulting from the effects of slope, wetness, soil texture, soil depth, plant growth deficiencies, stones, etc. Normally the limitations can be overcome with correct planning, careful design, and good management.

3. Severe soil limitations—Soils with severe limitations resulting from the effects of steep slopes, high water table, stream flooding, unfaborable soil texture, acidity, large numbers of stones, rocks, etc. Soils rated as having a severe limitation are severe enough to make the use of the soil doubtful for the proposed use. Careful planning and above-average design and management are required. This often includes major soil reclamation work.

When five interpretive groupings are used instead of three the soils are rated as having none, slight, moderate, severe, and very severe limitations. Essentially this involves dividing the first and last groups in the three class system.

Table 1. Soil limitations for camp areas (Intensive use).*

Soil items affecting use	Degree of soil limitation		
	None to slight	Moderate	Severe
Wetness	Well to moderately well drained soils with no ponding and with water table below 3 feet	Moderately well drained soils with water table less than 3 feet and somewhat poorly drained soils with no ponding	Well drained, moderately well drained and somewhat poorly, with occasional ponding of short duration, poorly, and very poorly drained soils
Flooding	None	None	Subject to flooding during season of use
Permeability†	Very rapid to moderate	Moderately slow	Slow and very slow
Slope	0-8%	8-15%	15% +
Surface soil texture	sl, fsl, vfsl, l, and ls with textural B horizon. Not subject to soil blowing	cl, scl, sicl, sil, ls, and sand other than loose sand	Organic, c, sic, c, loose sand, and soils subject to severe blowing.
Coarse fragments < 10"	Less than 15%	15-50%	50% +
Stoniness or rockiness‡	None	Classes 1 and 2	Classes 3, 4, and 5

* Based on soil limitations during use season. † In low rainfall areas soils may be rated one class better. ‡ For definitions see Soil Survey Manual, pp. 217-221.

Table 2. Soil limitations for buildings in recreational areas.*

Soil items affecting use	Degree of soil limitation		
	None to slight	Moderate	Severe†
Wetness	Well to moderately well drained soils not subject to ponding or seepage Over 4 feet to seasonal water table	Well and moderately well drained soils subject to occasional ponding or seepage Somewhat poorly drained not subject to ponding. Seasonal water table 2-4 feet ‡	Somewhat poorly drained soils subject to ponding. Poorly and very poorly drained soils
Flooding	Not subject to flooding	Not subject to flooding	Subject to flooding
Slope	0-8%	8-15%	15% +
Rockiness§	Class 0	Class 1	Classes 2, 3, 4, and 5
Stoniness§	Classes 0 and 1	Class 2	Classes 3, 4, and 5
Depth to hard bedrock	5 feet +	3-5 feet‡	Less than 3 feet

* Soil limitations for septic tank filter fields, hillside slippage, frost heave, piping, loose sand, and low bearing capacity when wet are items not included in this rating that must be considered. Soil ratings for these items have been developed.
† Soils rated as having severe soil limitations for individual cottage sites may be best from an aesthetic or use standpoint but they do require more preparation or maintenance for such use. ‡ These items are limitations only where basements and underground utilities are planned. § Based on definitions in Soil Survey Manual, pp. 217-221.

Table 3. Soil limitations for play areas (Intensive use).

Soil items affecting use	Degree of soil limitation		
	None to slight	Moderate	Severe
Wetness	Well and moderately well drained soils with no ponding or seepage	Well and moderately well drained soils subject to occasional ponding or seepage of short duration. Somewhat poorly drained soils	Somewhat poorly subject to ponding, poorly, and very poorly drained soils. Too wet for use for periods of 1-5 weeks during season of use
Flooding	None during season of use	Subject to occasional flooding. Not more than once in 3 years	Subject to more than occasional flooding during season of use
Permeability*	Rapid, moderately rapid and moderate	Moderately slow	Slow and very slow
Slope	0-2%	2-8%	8% +
Surface soil texture	sl, fsl, vfsl, l and ls with textural B horizon	cl, scl, sicl, sil, ls, and sand	sc, sic, c, organic soils and sand and loamy sand subject to blowing
Depth to hard bedrock	3 feet +	2-3 feet†	Less than 2 feet
Stoniness‡	Class 0	Classes 1 and 2	Classes 3, 4, and 5
Rockiness	None	Class 1	Classes 2, 3, 4, and 5
Coarse fragments	Free of coarse fragments	Up to 15% coarse fragments	15% +

* In arid regions soils may be rated one class better. † These soils have severe limitations if slope is greater than 2%. ‡ As per definitions in Soil Survey Manual, pp 217-221.

The guides set forth in Tables 1, 2, 3, 4, and 5 are suggested for use in developing soil interpretations for picnic areas, intensive play areas, buildings in recreational areas, intensive camp areas, and for paths and trails.*

These guides are useful in evaluating each kind of soil to be grouped into soil limitation classes for different recreational uses. It is recognized that interactions, in different major land resource areas, among some of the soil qualities listed in these guides may be great enough to change the soil limitation rating by one class. Soils having the same soil name and occurring in the same land resource area normally will have the same rating.

It is not anticipated that all of these interpretations will be needed in all areas. Interpretations for other recreational uses should be developed locally as needed.

It is important that the proper perspective be placed on the use of soil interpretations in recreational planning. They are based on

*Credit is given to a number of soil scientists in the Soil Conservation Service who developed early drafts of these guides.

Table 4. Soil limitations for paths and trails.

Soil items affecting use	Degree of soil limitation		
	None to slight	Moderate	Severe
Wetness*	Well and moderately well drained soils with seasonal water table below 3 feet	Well and moderately well drained soils subject to seepage or ponding and somewhat poorly drained soils. Seasonal water table 1-3 feet	Poorly drained and very poorly drained soils
Flooding*	Not subject to flooding during season of use	Subject to occasional flooding. May flood 1 or 2 times during season of use	Frequent flooding during season of use
Slope†	0-15%	15-25%	25% +
Surface texture‡	sl, fsl, vfsl, l	sil, sicl, scl, cl, sc, ls	sic, c, sand, and soils subject to severe blowing
	Gravelly and non-gravelly		All very gravelly, very cherty, very cobbly, very channery soils
Surface stoniness or rockiness§	Classes 0, 1, and 2	Class 3	Classes 4 and 5

* Season of use should be considered in evaluating these items. † Soil erodibility is an important item to evaluate in rating this item. Some adjustments in slope range may be needed in different climatic zones. ‡ In arid and subhumid climates some of the finer textured soils may be reduced one soil limitation class. § Based on definitions in Soil Survey Manual, pp. 217-221.

Table 5. Soil limitations for picnic areas (Intensive use).

Soil items affecting use	Degree of soil limitation		
	None to slight	Moderate	Severe
Wetness	Well and moderately well drained soils not subject to ponding	Well drained, moderately well drained soil subject to occasional ponding. Somewhat poorly drained not subject to ponding	Poorly drained & very poorly drained soils. Somewhat poorly drained soils subject to ponding. Too wet for use for periods of more than 4 weeks during season of use
Flooding	None during season of use	May flood 1 or 2 times for short period during season of use	Floods more than 2 to 4 times during season of use
Slope	0-8%	8-15%	15% +
Surface soil texture	sl, fsl, vfsl, l and ls with textural B. Not subject to blowing	cl, scl, sicl, sil, ls, and sand other than loose sand. *	sc, sic, c, s, organic. soils and soils subject to severe blowing.
Stoniness†	Classes 0, 1, and 2	Class 3	Classes 4 and 5
Rockiness	Classes 0, 1, and 2	Class 3	Classes 4 and 5

* In arid and subhumid climates fine textured soils may be classified as having a moderate limitation. † See definition in Soil Survey Manual, pp. 217-221.

soil features only and do not include other factors such as location, aesthetic values, and nearness to population centers. A soil survey properly interpreted is a useful guide for general recreation planning and in site selection, planning, and design of recreational facilities.

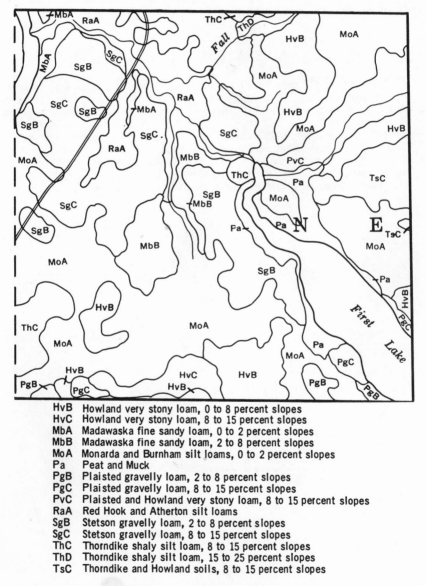

HvB	Howland very stony loam, 0 to 8 percent slopes
HvC	Howland very stony loam, 8 to 15 percent slopes
MbA	Madawaska fine sandy loam, 0 to 2 percent slopes
MbB	Madawaska fine sandy loam, 2 to 8 percent slopes
MoA	Monarda and Burnham silt loams, 0 to 2 percent slopes
Pa	Peat and Muck
PgB	Plaisted gravelly loam, 2 to 8 percent slopes
PgC	Plaisted gravelly loam, 8 to 15 percent slopes
PvC	Plaisted and Howland very stony loam, 8 to 15 percent slopes
RaA	Red Hook and Atherton silt loams
SgB	Stetson gravelly loam, 2 to 8 percent slopes
SgC	Stetson gravelly loam, 8 to 15 percent slopes
ThC	Thorndike shaly silt loam, 8 to 15 percent slopes
ThD	Thorndike shaly silt loam, 15 to 25 percent slopes
TsC	Thorndike and Howland soils, 8 to 15 percent slopes

Figure 1. Soil map of 1,000-acre tract of land - Aroostock County, Maine.

The maps in Figure 1 and in Plates 13 to 17 (pages 192 to 196) illustrate how these guides are applied to a 1,000-acre tract of land to show the degree of soil limitation for various uses of the different soils. Figure 1 is a soil survey map of the area. The Plates show the interpretation of the soils information based on five different proposed recreational uses.

LITERATURE CITED

1. Soil Survey Staff. 1960. Soil Classification, A Comprehensive System, 7th Approximation. Soil Conservation Service, USDA.
2. Soil Survey Staff. 1951. Soil Survey Manual. USDA Handbook No. 18, Washington, D.C.
3. Bender, William H. 1961. Soils suitable for septic tank filter fields. USDA Agriculture Information Bull. No. 243.
4. Allan, Philip F., Garland, Lloyd E., and Dunga, R. Franklin. 1963. Rating northeastern soils for their suitability for wildlife habitat. Trans. 28th North American Wildlife and Natural Resources Conf.

CHAPTER 11

IMPROVING SOIL SURVEY INTERPRE-TATIONS THROUGH RESEARCH

Gerald W. Olson[1]

RESEARCH IN SOIL SURVEY interpretations seeks ways to improve use of soil maps and reports. Intensive use of soil surveys as resource inventories[15,18] necessitates that we learn more about soils and their performance. To acquire this information, soil scientists who make soil maps need to combine forces with planners, engineers, and others who use soil maps.

This paper gives examples of the nature of an interdisciplinary approach to soil research, including an example of its application to problems of subsurface sewage disposal.

SOIL SURVEY

Interdisciplinary contributions have helped make study of soils a science. Many fields such as geology, geography, meteorology, botany, and chemistry have contributed to understanding of factors and processes that have formed soils. Soils, an integral part of our environment, are discrete bodies produced by interactions of climate and vegetation changing surficial geologic materials in geomorphic landscapes.

Interdisciplinary work is as important in application of soil information for practical purposes as it is in understanding theories of soil genesis. To build structures on soils, knowledge of soil characteristics must be combined with knowledge of planning, engineering, design, economics, and other disciplines that study man's use of land, in order to achieve harmonious and efficient land use.

A soil scientist making a soil map studies soil color, texture, structure, porosity, consistence, pH, organic matter, kind of clay, and other profile characteristics, and combines these with his knowledge of geomorphology, topography, vegetation, land use, and other landscape attributes to delineate different soil areas on maps.[22] Soil map units are clearly defined in soil survey reports and can be used with confidence by planners and developers. In

---

1. Soil Technologist, Cornell University, Ithaca, N. Y. Cornell Agronomy Paper No. 695.

some cases, however, experience and data are lacking and greater detail of study of certain soil properties is necessary. For example, slope and drainage are very important soil characteristics for many urban uses. In street layout, highly detailed soil slope and topographic maps are helpful for city planning. Detailed studies of drainage and water table fluctuations in soils are ncesssary where certain wet soils are to be reclaimed for urban development.

RESEARCH ON RELATIONSHIPS BETWEEN MAN AND SOILS

Relationships between man and soils are little understood and have not been adequately studied. Literature of anthropology, planning, geography, economics, ecology, and other disciplines contains many allusions to influence of soils on man.[1,24,29] Man's actions have been channeled by natural features of the land since he appeared on the earth. Soil as support and nurture of man is worthy of further study because, even in cities, man depends to a large extent upon soil for food, support, waste disposal, and many raw materials. If we knew more about man-soil relationships, we would probably be better able to plan for the future.

Road patterns generally illustrate influence of soil features upon man's activities. Highway 104 along Lake Ontario in New York State follows beach ridges of old glacial lakes for most of its length. It is called "Ridge Road." The highway and adjacent houses and villages are located along the ridges because the old beach ridges are sandy and gravelly and better drained than most of the rest of the lake plain. Similarly, sandy and gravelly glacial deltas are sites of many villages. Roads follow eskers, outwash deposits, deltas, and beach ridges in many parts of New York State. In the Allegheny Plateau region, level gravelly outwash valleys support prosperous agriculture, villages, and industry, and provide major avenues for roads and railroads. Plateau areas of poorer soils between the valleys support only forests in many places.

Archeological evidence suggests that, in some ways, primitive man was a better selector of sites for building than modern man. He seems to have been more aware of the natural environment about him. Some building sites today are selected on the basis of political or economic decisions alone. Many times contractors develop tracts they own or can easily obtain, without regard to alternative site development of places with better soil characteristics. Sometimes serious mistakes are made. For example, annual urban losses from flooding of alluvial areas illustrate that soil information, properly interpreted, can be very valuable in planning and zoning floodplain areas.

One example of use of soil information in trying to interpret man's relationship to the environment is found in the anthropological studies of Tikal, site of the largest ceremonial city of the Maya civilization, in Guatemala. Hundreds of remains of centers of ceremony, government, artisanship, and residence prove that this civilization, which fluorished from about 200 to 900 A. D., was very advanced.[4] Scientists have proposed that the civilization declined because of soil depletion and erosion. Warnings like this must be taken seriously for future planning.[13] Some soil studies have been undertaken to investigate this hypothesis.[5,6]

Maps of the Tikal ruins show remarkable correlation of ruins with soils.[2] Ruins of buildings are concentrated on the upland soils and avoid the swampy soils. Present urban development northwest of New York City[26] similarly avoids swampy soil areas. The cluster developments at Tikal also have patterns similar to cluster developments of modern cities.[28] Tikal planners and architects apparently knew a great deal about use of the best soils for construction purposes, and about spatial arrangement of buildings on them.

RESEARCH ON SOIL MAP UNITS

Many people other than soil scientists examine soils. For example, highway engineers dig deep test holes for bridge footings and road excavations. The borings are logged on engineering diagrams. Each boring applies only to that site. If the boring data are correlated with the soil map units, however, the value of the data is multiplied many times through predictive use. When a large amount of data is accumulated, soil characteristics such as depth to bedrock can be established within narrowly defined limits for each map unit. This kind of data is easiest to correlate when soil scientists and highway engineers work together to interpret deep borings and relate them to areas of soil map units.

Well logs illustrate another area of research opportunity. Very valuable data about materials and depth to groundwater can be obtained as wells are drilled. The data should be carefully recorded so that observations can be interpreted by soil scientists and groundwater geologists. If this information is related to specific soil map units, it has predictive value for all areas of the same map units. The more data available, the more accurate the predictions. In most soil surveys this information is not available to soil scientists, and only general statements can be made for each soil map unit regarding deep substrata and groundwater.

Public health officials conduct many percolation tests in soils to assess capacity to absorb effluent from septic tank seepage fields. Generally, the percolation test rates are not related to soil map units. If soils are carefully described during interdisciplinary work by public health engineers and soil scientists,[16] and if results of percolation tests are carefully logged, the data can be used to accurately predict percolation rates in each soil map unit.

Planners need to understand soil map units because the units, or groupings of them, separate soil characteristics that are significant for land use. For example, planners using soil maps can delineate areas that are shallow to bedrock, steep, wet, or flooded. Similarly, planners can locate soil areas that are permeable, have good grading characteristics, and are good potential industrial sites. Planners can also contribute their knowledge of how the maps are used for planning to soil scientists, who in turn can make the map units more reliable to show special soil properties important for planning. Research on soil map units can be designed to determine statistical reliability of soil and inclusions within each map unit. Some soil map units are homogenous; others are more heterogeneous.

Most disciplines that deal with man's use of land can benefit from correlating their data with soil map units. For example, an economic study in the Allegheny Plateau region of New York State showed striking differences in incomes of dairy farms on hill and valley landscapes.[7] Comparative average income from hill farms on till soils was only about 60% of income from valley farms on outwash soils. These income differences have profound effects upon prosperity of entire communities. Correlations of economic differences such as these with soil map units would be useful in influencing planning decisions for the future. In most cases agriculture should not be encouraged in, or possibly even should be zoned out of, soil areas where economic studies show that farming is unprofitable. Such planning foresight could alleviate much human suffering and economic loss and enable land to be used more efficiently.

RESEARCH ON MAP CORRELATIONS

Soil maps need to be correlated with other maps. Maps of New York State show good examples of soil relationships mapped on a small scale that should be further investigated and correlated on maps at larger scales. Figure 1 is a map of New York soil groups that show important characteristics and mode of deposition. The outwash soils are sandy or gravelly. They are generally good for urban development and have good groundwater supplies. The other

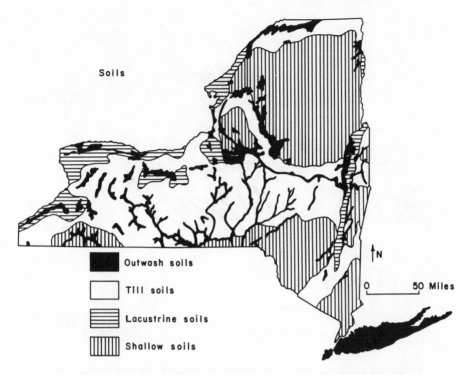

Figure 1. General groups of soils of New York State (adapted from Cline, 1963; Feuer et al., 1963).

soils have poor groundwater supplies. Figure 2 was drawn from a map made by groundwater geologists, more or less independently of soils information. Figures 1 and 2 show remarkable agreement, particularly for the outwash soils that have good groundwater yields. These soils have a great influence on urban development and economic progress (Figure 3). Although many factors other than soils are involved in economic health of areas shown in Figure 3, it is no accident that many of the prosperous communities are located on permeable outwash soils with good construction properties and good groundwater yields.

Relief is one of the factors of soil formation, and is reflected in a map of geomorphic regions of New York State. Soils of the lowlands (Figure 4) in New York State, in general, have many more desirable properties for intensive development than do soils of the highlands with rugged topography. For this reason the major transportation routes (Figure 5) follow the lowlands (Figure 4) where the most favorable topography and construction materials (Figure 1)

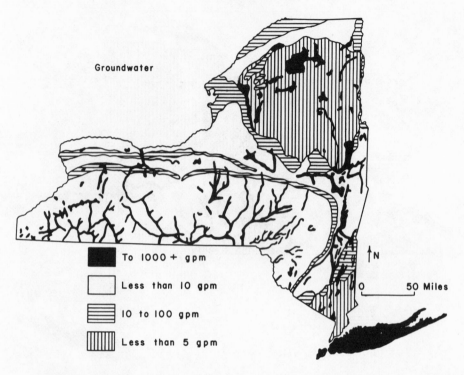

Figure 2. General groundwater yields in New York State (adapted from Health, 1964; USGS, 1962).

are located. Similarly, the urban centers of economic activity (Figure 3) are generally located on the best soils of the best topography with the best groundwater resources (Figure 2). Urban areas are located where transportation is easy and rapid to other urban centers; they generally occupy best locations along major transportation routes. Neither transportation routes (Figure 5) nor urban centers (Figure 3) developed first—they developed concurrently and supplemented each other, primarily located as they are due to naturally favorable environmental conditions, including soils.

The same relationships shown on maps in Figures 1-5 are more accurately delineated on larger scale maps. It is important that soil scientists, groundwater geologists, economists, geomorphologists, highway engineers, and others get together in studying and compiling their maps in order to make them more useful. Thus maps like those of Figures 1-5 show very close relationships— where differences exist they are largely due to cartographic groupings and inclusions within each map unit. If the original maps had

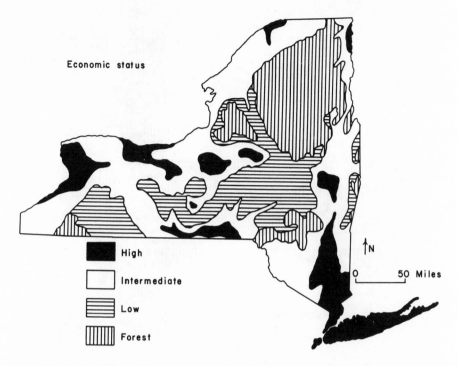

Figure 3. General economic status of areas of New York State (adapted from Sufrin et al., 1960; Thompson et al., 1962).

been prepared cooperatively, instead of independently, they would show even more accurate correlations.

Planners can use map correlations to great benefit. Planning reports generally bring together many useful separate maps showing urban area growth, land use, geology, topography, soils, drainage, population, traffic patterns, proposed development, and other urban area attributes. If these maps can be related to one another, possibly on the same scale with overlays, they can be more meaningful for users of planning reports.

RESEARCH FOR SUBSURFACE SEWAGE DISPOSAL IN SOILS OF BROOME COUNTY, NEW YORK

The Binghamton urban area in Broome County in the Allegheny Plateau region of New York State has particularly well-defined relationships (Figures 1-5) between soils and urban development,

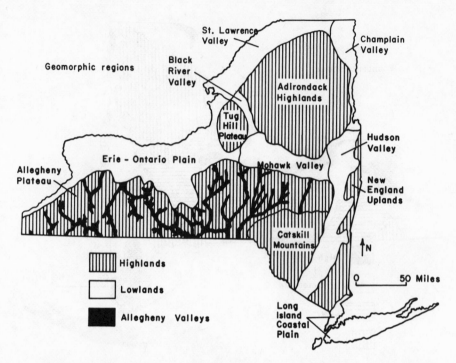

Figure 4. General geomorphic regions of New York State (adapted from Cline, 1963).

primarily because of the nature of the glacial materials, geomorphology, slope, and drainage. The board level valleys have deep deposits of gravelly outwash soils (excellent for urban development) and the hills have impermeable till soils that are shallow to shale bedrock in many places (poor for urban development). General relationships of some of the major soils around Binghamton are illustrated in Figure 6. Binghamton is so located (Figure 3) in the Allegheny Plateau (Figure 4) primarily because the broad level valleys of gravely outwash soils (Figure 1) permitted good transportation routes (Figure 5) to an area with good groundwater resources for industry (Figure 2).

Planners in Broome County were the first to realize that general soil maps, though very useful,[14,20] were not adequate to meet all the needs for detail in planning for rapidly expanding suburban areas around Binghamton. In addition the planners investigated possibilities for making detailed soil maps more accurate with supplemental research, particularly for subsurface sewage disposal in areas without public sewers.

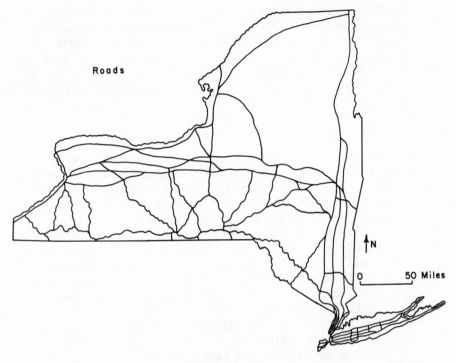

Figure 5. General transportation routes (roads) in New York State (adapted from several current road maps).

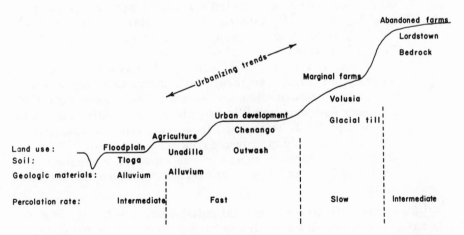

Figure 6. General relationships of some of the major soils of Broome County, New York, to geologic material, landscape position, percolation rate, land use, and urbanizing trends.

The Board of Supervisors in Broome County recognized that the soil map at a scale of four to one mile could be made much more accurate for subsurface sewage disposal with supplemental inter-disciplinary soil research, conducted in cooperation with the Planning Board, Health Department, Extension Service, and Soil Conservation Service. Consequently a grant was made to the Department of Agronomy of Cornell University to study the soils of Broome County specifically for subsurface sewage disposal.[10,11,17] This project consisted of the following aspects:

1. Percolation tests were made at many sites in most soils of Broome County. On the basis of the percolation test results,[10] the soils were classified into groups. By statistical analysis of the data, a percolation rate for seepage field design was determined for each of the soil groups.

2. Water table fluctuations were measured for two years. The behavior of water tables in different soils was used as additional criteria for design of seepage fields. These measurements are being continued by the Health Department to provide data for future soil interpretations covering longer periods of climatic variations.

3. A statistical, random sampling of subsurface sewage disposal systems in current use in different soils was made. The incidence of failures and successes and probable causes of both in different soils were determined as further criteria for seepage field designs.

4. On the basis of data collected during soil survey and soil research, soils of Broome County were classified into sets of soil conditions[11] upon which designs for septic tank seepage fields were based.

5. In cooperation with county, state, and federal public health officials and other engineers and individuals, designs for subsurface sewage disposal seepage fields were specified for each soil map unit.[17] In general, three different kinds of seepage fields were used in accord with soil characteristics, research, and proven engineering designs.[19,21] Variations of the three designs were necessary for steep slopes, flooded areas, and large flat areas without adequate surface drainage.

Soil research data showed that soils of Broome County (Figure 6) have very different capacities to handle septic tank effluent (Figure 7). Variations in soil properties causing these performance differences occur within short distances, as shown on the soil map. For example (Figure 7), Chenango soils are very permeable and

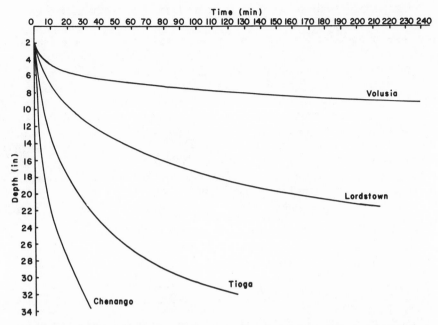

Figure 7. Percolation test curves (water level drop in presoaked holes) illustrative of some of the major soils of Broome County, New York, shown in Figure 6. (Each curve represents data from several holes at one site, idealized from Huddleston, 1965a, p. 46-49, 88-90, 173-174, 272-274.)

seepage fields with tile lines in gravel can be used in them according to standard design curves.[19] Nearby Volusia soils, however, are practically impermeable below the topsoil due to a dense fragipan and compact till. Volusia soils need artificial sand filters that do not use the natural soil for absorption. Other soils, like Lordstown and Tioga, are shallow to bedrock or flooded. For subsurface sewage disposal, they need to have seepage fields in specified loamy fill.[21]

The research information, developed in cooperation with all interested agencies and individuals, is being implemented through community action groups working with the Broome County Planning Board, Health Department, and Extension Service. From the soil map, a person interested in building a home on a specific lot can tell what kind of seepage field he will need for subsurface sewage disposal simply by identifying the soil map unit within which his lot is located, and relating the map unit to the seepage field design prescribed for it. This can be done without visiting the site, with an accuracy probably better than 90%. Greater accuracy can be achieved with on-site soil examinations and percolation tests.

The study in Broome County is an effort to combine intensive interdisciplinary soil research with engineering tests and designs for subsurface sewage disposal, to achieve reliable predictive use of the detailed soil map on aerial photographs at a scale of four inches to one mile. The research enabled designs for seepage fields to be recommended for entire map units, not just for the one site at which a percolation test or soil examination was made.

The Broome County study was an example study. Other soil problems of the increasing population can be solved by using similar analysis of data in application to specific soil map units. With larger scale soil maps, the research data can be made even more reliable.[12] Thus data of planners, engineers, groundwater geologists, economists, anthropologists, and many others can be applied to specific soil map units to give very accurate predictive value to soil maps.

LITERATURE CITED

1. Butzer, K. W. 1960. Archeology and geology in ancient Egypt. Science 132:1617-1624.
2. Carr, R. F. and J.E. Hazard. 1961. Map of the ruins of Tikal, El Peten, Guatemala. University of Pennsylvania Museum Monographs Report No. 11.
3. Cline, M. G. 1963 (Reprinted). Soils and soil associations of New York. Cornell University Extension Bulletin No. 930.
4. Coe, W. R. 1965. Tikal, Guatemala, and emergent Maya civilization. Science 147:1401-1419.
5. Cowgill, U. M. 1961. Soil fertility and the ancient Maya. Trans. Connecticut Acad. Arts and Sciences 42:1-56.
6. Cowgill, U. M., et al. 1963. El Bajo de Santa Fe. Trans. Philosophical Soc. 53:1-51.
7. Cunningham, L. C. 1961. Commercial dairy farming in the Plateau Region of New York, 1957-58. Cornell University Agr. Exp. Sta. Bull. No. 966.
8. Feuer, R., et al. 1963 (Reprinted). New York agriculture at a glance. New York State College of Agriculture.
9. Heath, R. C. 1964. Groundwater in New York. State of New York Conservation Department Water Resources Commission Bull. No. GW-51.
10. Huddleston, J. H. 1965a. Data assembled for soil survey interpretation for subsurface sewage disposal in Broome County, New York. Cornell University Agronomy Mimeo No. 65 - 19.
11. Huddleston, J. H. 1965b. Soil survey interpretation for subsurface sewage disposal in Broome County, New York. Cornell University M. Sc. Thesis.
12. Huddleston, J. H. and G. W. Olson. 1963. Urban soil survey of the village of Whitney Point, New York: An example study showing the direct application of soil survey toward solution of a village's sewage disposal problems. Cornell University Department of Agronomy.

13. Lowdermilk, W. C. 1953. Conquest of the land through seven thousand years. USDA, Soil Conservation Service, Agr. Information Bull. No. 99.
14. Montillon, E. D. 1964. Rural Broome County. Broome County Planning Board.
15. Olson, G. W. 1964a. Application of soil survey to problems of health, sanitation, and engineering. Cornell University Memoir No. 387.
16. Olson, G. W. 1964b. Using soil surveys for problems of the expanding population in New York State. Cornell University Extension Bull. No. 1123.
17. Olson, G. W., et al. 1965. Designs of seepage fields for subsurface sewage disposal in soils of Broome County, New York. Cornell University Agronomy Mimeo No. 65 - 20.
18. Orvedal, A. C. 1963. The seventh approximation: Its application in engineering. Soil Science 96:62-67.
19. PHS. 1963 (Reprinted). Manual of septic tank practice. U. S. Public Health Service Publ. No. 526.
20. Prokosch, W., et al. 1963. Comprehensive plan for Broome County to 1980. Prepared by Tippetts - Abbett - McCarthy - Stratton, consulting architects and engineers, for Broome County Planning Board.
21. Salvato, J. A., Jr. 1958. Environmental sanitation. John Wiley and Sons, Inc.
22. Stephens, C. G. 1953. Soil surveys for land development. Food and Agriculture Organization of the United Nations Agr. Studies No. 20.
23. Sufrin, S. C., et al. 1960. The economic status of upstate New York at midcentury with special reference to distressed communities and their adjustments. Business Research Center of Syracuse University.
24. Thomas, W. L., Jr. (Editor) et al. 1956. Man's role in changing the face of the earth. The University of Chicago Press.
25. Thompson, J. H., et al. 1962. Toward a geography of economic health: The case of New York State. Annals Assoc. Amer. Geographers 52:1-20.
26. USGS. 1947. Topographic map of Newark quadrangle at scale of 1:250,000. U. S. geological Survey Map No. 18-11.
27. USGS. 1962. Water resource investigations in New York. U. S. Geological Survey.
28. Whyte, W. H. 1964. Cluster development. American Conservation Association.
29. Zobler, L. 1957. Statistical testing of regional boundaries. Annals Assoc. Amer. Geographers 47:83-95.

CHAPTER 12

THE URBAN SOILS PROGRAM IN PRINCE WILLIAM COUNTY, VIRGINA

Dwight L. Kaster and Oscar W. Yates, Jr.

A COOPERATIVE DETAILED soil survey agreement was made and initiated in 1958 between the Prince William County Board of Supervisors, the Agronomy Department of Virginia Polytechnic Institute, and the USDA Soil Conservation Service. This soil survey was designed for anticipated urban as well as for agriculture uses. After the soil survey was completed, the soils maps were redrafted on cronaflex to facilitate copying for public distribution (milar where maps can be copied by ammonia processing method on the county Ozolid machine). It is now possible for the public of obtain at a nominal fee the aerial mosaics, base maps, tax maps showing various parcels of land in the county and type of zoning, and the soils maps at a scale of 1" = 400'. Consequently, information is easily transferable from one map to another.

After the mapping was completed a popularized soils report was written for each soil type within the county. This popularized report included a short description of each soil type, suitability of each soil type for engineering or urban uses as well as various agriculture and forestry uses and the more significant problems likely to be encountered with each soil type in these various uses as reflected by their physical characteristics. Consequently, any person or agency can acquire a copy of the soils map and interpretative material for all or any portion or parcel of land in Prince William County.

After completion of the soil survey map and the soils report, an agreement between the Board of Supervisors of Prince William County and the Agronomy Department of Virginia Polytechnic Institute was made whereby the Agronomy Department would furnish a staff employee to remain in the county to make on site investigations and interpret soils information for specific urban uses. This soil scientist is technically responsible to the Agronomy Department and administratively responsible in county affairs to the Prince William County Public Works Department. For the soil scientist's services, Prince William County agreed to pay the Agronomy Department of Virginia Polytechnic Institute a portion of his salary

---

1. Virginia Polytechnic Institute and Prince William County, Virginia.

and most of his expenses. Although the soil scientist works out of the Public Works Department which is the center of activity and co-ordinator for site plans, subdivision plans, etc., he serves all county departments upon request.

The majority of his work is with the Public Works Department, County Health Department, Planning Department, County School Board, County Department of Revenue, and the Sanitary Districts for the County. The Operations Division of the Public Works Department is the coordinator of subdivisions and site plans submitted to the County by developers.

It is their responsibility to distribute the subdivision and site plans to each department or agency concerned for processing. After processing, the Operations Division presents the subdivision and site plans with comments of each department or agency to the County Board of Supervisors for approval or rejection. As the Soils Division of the Public Works Department, the Soil Scientist reviews these plans and makes comments relative to suitability of the soils in these areas for foundations, road building materials, or individual absorption fields for sewage disposal systems.

The Soil Scientist is often requested by the Building Division of the Public Works Department to make on site investigations or problem soils and submit a written report as to the suitability of this soil for the proposed building before construction is permitted.

The Engineering Division of the Public Works Department is responsible for all subdivision roads or streets meeting the State Highway Department specifications or the equivalent. This division has installed a County Soil Mechanics laboratory to run compaction (proctor and field density tests) liquid and plastic limits, seive sizes or particle distribution, volume changes, etc. The Soil Scientist has use of the laboratory and an annual budget for equipment needed to carry on research on soils related to urban development. At present, we are trying to correlate soils mechanics laboratory results with soil types.

The Soil Scientist collaborates with the County Health Department on the suitability of soils for individual absorption fields for sewage disposal systems for subdivisions, site plans and individual houses in rural areas. If a large area such as a subdivision is involved he makes an on site investigation with the Sanitarian and presents a detailed soils map of the area and the accompanied interpretative material to the Health Department. If only a single lot is involved he makes an on site investigation with the sanitarian and writes a report on soil conditions on this lot relative to their suitability for septic tank absorption fields.

The Planning Department of Prince William County requested

upon completion of the detailed soils map a generalized or soil association map of the county to be used as an aid in developing a master plan for the county. They requested each soil association be rated generally as to their suitability for important urban uses. More detailed soils maps and interpretative information is often requested by the Planning Department in zoning cases to be submitted to the Planning Commission.

The County Department of Revenue also requested detailed soil maps of the entire county and interpretative information on all soil types to be used as an aid in reassessment of all parcels of land in the county for taxation.

The County School Board in the various districts request the Soil Scientist to make on site investigations of proposed school sites and submit a detailed soils map and interpretative information to the Board relative to suitability of the soils for foundations, road building materials, parking lots, and in rural areas septic tank absorption fields.

The Soil Scientist receives requests from the Sanitary Districts to supply information on depth to hard rock as related to routine of sewer lines, suitability of soils for footings for water tanks and on site investigations on proposed sewage disposal systems. They are interested in information such as seasonal water tables, susceptibility of the site of flooding, and ease in moving soil or rock formations in construction of these disposal systems.

The Agronomy Department of Virginia Polytechnic Institute, Prince William County, and the State Health Department are now making plans to start water table studies in colluvial soils and soils with slowly permeable horizons. The Public Works Department and the Agronomy Department also plan to run bearing tests on the subsoils and parent materials or substrates of the dominant soil types in the county. There is need for more accurate data than is now available in ranges in bearing values within and between dominant soil types. This will help immensely in predicting general presumptive bearing values of soil types throughout the county.

With a good detailed soils map at 1" = 400' and by making site soil investigations the soils program in Prince William County is generally sound. There is need however for much more specific information on soil water relationships especially in parent materials and substratas. There is need for more soil mechanics laboratory data on liquid limits, plastic indexes, volume changes, wet and dry densities, presumptive bearing values, etc., within and between soil types. The job of the soil scientist in Prince William County is to predict the behavior of soils under various urban uses and the more accurate information we can collect the more accurate are our predictions.

CHAPTER 13

A "SYSTEM" OF SOIL SURVEY, INTERPRETATION, EDUCATION, AND USE

W. J. Meyer,[1] W. H. Bender,[2] K. A. Wenner,[3] and J. Rinier[4]

SOIL SURVEY INFORMATION evolves from exacting field and laboratory studies. The usefulness of this information is entirely dependent upon interpretations which need to be transmitted and explained to potential users by intense educational programs. In this way soil information can be applied most successfully by those concerned with using the soil in an economical and logical manner.

The objective of a field study is to record data on the soils of a specific area. This includes the separation of the landscape into soil mapping units, and describing these units in quantitative and qualitative terms. The data are based on the fact that individual kinds of soil re-occur in the landscape within the framework of a given set of conditions governed by the forces of climate, vegetation and relief acting on parent material over a period of time. The soil is a result of these forces. It must be separated into meaningful units and described for interpretative and predictive purposes.

Separations of soil mapping units are based on soil characteristics including the sequence and thickness of soil horizons and the color, texture, structure, and consistence of the material

1. Assistant Agronomist, Virginia Polytechnic Institute, assigned to the Division of Local Health Services, Virginia State Health Dept. as Soil Consultant.

2. Soil Scientist, South Regional Technical Service Center, Soil Conservation Service, USDA, Forth Worth, Texas.

3. County Extension Agent in Soils, Indiana Cooperative Extension Service, Crown Point, Ind.

4. Professor of Geography, Kent State University, Kent, Ohio.

This article is a condensation of papers presented by the above authors as a panel discussion at a joint meeting of Divisions A-2, A-4, and S-5 of the American Society of Agronomy, Columbus, Ohio, November 1965. It was prepared by Milford R. Heddleson, Extension Agronomist, The Pennsylvania State University, University Park, Pa.

in each horizon. Geology, drainage, and geomorphology strongly influence the occurrence of different soil mapping units. Borings into the soil profile permit observation of the soil characteristics which can eventually be more accurately associated with what is more readily observable from the soil surface. Patterns of natural bodies on the landscape emerge and these boundaries are recorded on aerial photographs of that particular landscape.

Complete detailed soil dscriptions are the basic informationn necessary to identify the samples upon which chemical, physical and mineralogical analyses can be accomplished. These combined data can then be used to obtain a quantitative measure of the soil resources of a landscape. The interpretations concerning the capabilities and limitations of the soils are based on these findings which may suggest the most logical and profitable use for the soil.

Genetic classifications considering all soil properties are useful in determining world-wide soil resources. Interpretations of soils are numerous depending upon specific fields of interest. Cropland interpretations consider such properties as fertility, drainage, slope, texture and structure in attaining groupings of soils suitable for specific agricultural uses. Engineering application criteria may emphasize depth to bedrock, water tables, permeability, stability, and shrink-swell potential in a soil classification to be used by engineers. Similarly, woodland, rangeland, recreational land, and land undergoing urban development require interpretations that relate to specific limiting or favorable soil factors. By no means will a particular soil be ranked in the same relative position in every interpretation.

Many prospective users of soils information are not acquainted with soils, soil terminology, or how certain properties can influence the responses of soil to use. Educational programs are therefore necessary to encourage widespread use of soil surveys. Soil survey reports are of little value until they are put into use.

The goal of a soil survey educational program is to enlighten the public about different characteristics of soils of the area, the availability of soils information, and the many uses of the survey. Such an educational program is challenging because the public represents many different groups or segments of society with different interests, needs and goals. Therefore, to make the program effective, one must identify and understand each group and present the needed information to it on a personal basis with definite objectives in mind. The information can be presented through any of the media presently influencing the group, but it must satisfy the interests and needs in a brief and easily understood manner. This type of approach necessitates conducting numerous educational efforts simultaneously; but it is more effective than a "one-shot" approach in reaching the many specialized groups that need to know about and use soils information.

The list of potential "users" of soils information is long and varied, but includes engineers, road builders, utility firms, general contractors, planners, developers, realtors, bankers, sanitarians, farmers, homeowners, and prospective homeowners. These groups can be made aware of the existence of the survey through public media such as newspapers, radio, and television, but their understanding of its value, content, and use depends primarily on group meetings. These educational meetings must then be oriented to fit the needs of the specific group. Leaflets, pictures, monoliths, and field trips also have proven valuable as teaching aids and enable the user to more closely identify his problems in land use.

Since many nonfarm users of soils information are not familiar with soils, special efforts must be made to enable them to understand why such information is valuable to them. However, these nonfarm groups are rapidly becoming the most intense users of the information contained in the soil survey report. Local, county, and regional planners are quick to realize the value of such information and are readily using this in their planning efforts. Many serious and costly mistakes already have been avoided by using basic soils information. The general public is becoming more aware of the value of soils information in community development and use. Much is yet to accomplished in getting maximum value from existing information.

CHAPTER 14

USE OF SOIL SURVEYS IN THE EQUALIZATION OF TAX ASSESSMENTS

Robert R. Kinney[1]

BEFORE ATTEMPTING to discuss the use of soil surveys in the equalization of tax assessments I would like to try to demonstrate and define what is meant by tax equalization.

Table 1 shows information for three neighboring farms. They vary in size but have the same market value of $50,000 each and it is assumed they produce the same amount of income for the farmer. The tax district has an average level of assessment of 40% of market value and an annual tax rate of $30.00 per $1000 of assessed value.

Table 1. What is meant by tax equalization.

	Farm A	Farm B	Farm C
Acres	300	200	150
Market value	$50,000	$50,000	$50,000
Before equalization assessed value	$15,000	$20,000	$25,000
taxes	$ 450	$ 600	$ 750
After equalization assessed value	$20,000	$20,000	$20,000
taxes	$ 600	$ 600	$ 600

* Avg assessment level 40%: Tax rate $30.00/M.

Before tax equalization assessed values ranged from 20 to 50% of market value or $15,000 to $25,000 while taxes ranged from a low of $450.00 to a high of $750.00.

After equalization the assessed value for each farm was 40% of market value or $20,000 resulting in each farm paying equal taxes of $600.00 each.

The objective of tax equalization is to tax all properties at a uniform relation to value. Usually this is a form of market value generally defined as the price that the property would sell for on the open market between a willing buyer and seller.

---

1. Board of Tax Appeals, Department of Taxation, Columbus, Ohio.

Equalization is usually accomplished by an assessor, in our state the county auditor, appraising the properties in his district periodically though the use of staff assessors or professional appraisal companies.

A good assessment equalization program should have some of the following requirements.

1st: (Most important) The assessment must be uniform.

2nd: The resulting value should be one that can be readily defended and explained to the taxpayer.

3rd: The cost of the assessment must be economical.

Since this is a mass appraisal program that must be completed in a relative short time at a low cost, a detailed analysis of each property cannot be made. The assessor must use streamline versions of the three basic appraisal methods, i.e., the cost, the income, or the market approach.

Published soil surveys can be useful to the assessor in estimating land value since they incorporate a wealth of information that has been collected and correlated by experts. This information is usually classified in a logical manner with appropriate maps that aid in the identification of different soil areas. Modern surveys also provide information helpful in evaluating soils for use as residential subdivisions or other than normal agricultural purposes.

Some of the problems in the use of soil surveys are:

1. The lack of modern soil surveys for all areas. As money and personnel become available this situation will probably improve.

2. Lack of personnel trained in the use of soil surveys.

3. Human inertia in using available information. This is of course a difficult one to solve but part of this problem arises from the difficulty of interpreting soil survey information.

I believe this is due, in part, to different objectives. The extension agronomist is primarily interested in increased net return from crops. Another soil scientist is interested in the clay content of a given soil, etc. The assessor or appraiser is interested in translating the soil survey data into an expression of market value assuming typical usage and management of a given soil.

Also the mass of technical information tends to overwhelm the average assessor. On one farm there might be a large number of different soil types all intermixed into several soil complexes.

The assessor, because of lack of training and time, is unable to differentiate between these soil types but will usually price his land first according to land usage, such as tillable land, pasture, etc., and then by soil complexes in some cases.

Modern surveys have helped by providing more information on both typical and attainable yields for different soil types. If this information could be extended to typical soil associations or complexes it would be very helpful. Also needed is information on the management conditions that resulted in typical yields. Another suggestion is the correlation of production information by soil drainage classes in a given geological area.

Soil surveys are used in Ohio assessment practice, generally as a check on prices derived from market data. Usually sales information is collected as each farm is inspected. Deducting the estimated value of the improvements from the sale price provides an estimate of the land value. These land value estimates are then analyzed considering time of sale and other factors. Here the soil survey is useful in that it aids the assessor to arrive at the per acre price he will use for a specific soil area and farm. While far from perfect this method has the advantage that it is based on what people locally feel land is worth and also it gives weight to all factors of value as expressed by the market.

As an example, use has been made of a generalized soil map for a part of Champaign County in western Ohio. The tillable land prices that were used in a reappraisal made this year were superimposed. A close observation indicates that the land prices do follow the change in soil types, ranging from a low of $125 per acre in the less-productive Miami-Fox-Casco-Rodman association to the $300 on highly productive soils in the Westland-Fox-Tawas soil area.

A more intensive use was made in the 1963 appraisal of Paulding county. Land prices were determined, using sales and other information, for each type of soil. These soil types were then grouped as shown in Table 2. From a detailed soil map the percentage of each soil type on a farm was estimated. This was used to arrive at a weighted tillable land price per acre as shown in Table 3 for the actual farms. The $190 weighted price per acre was then multiplied by the number of tillable acres to arrive at the total value of the crop land on the farm.

While this method has been used in several counties this county auditor went a step further. He prepared a plat book showing on one side the soil map for a mile section of land and on the other side the owners and the value of the different tracts

Table 2. Condensed list of soil type prices.

Group	No. of soil types	Per acre price range
1	2	$50 to $65
2	2	$200 to $250
3	4	$85 to $250
4	1	$70 to $240
5	7	$150 to $250
6	6	$200 to $300
7	1	$280 to $300
8	1	$320

Table 3. Determination of tillable land price per acre taken from an actual appraisal card.

Soil group	Price per acre	%	Weight
1	$ 64	× 10 or	$ 6.40
2	$200	× 60 or	120.00
4	$200	× 25 or	50.00
6	$280	× 5 or	14.00
Weighted tillable land price per acre			$190.00

in the section. This was useful in a discussion of values with the taxpayer.

Another application is the use of production information from the surveys to extend sale information to soil types where there are no sales and to check the range of land prices for the different soil types as shown in Table 4.

Table 4. Example of use of soil surveys to establish a reasonable sale value of agricultural lands where sales records are nonexistent.

Crop	Unit price	Soil "A" Yield	Soil "A" Gross	Soil "B" Yield	Soil "B" Gross
Corn	$ 1.20	60 bu	$ 72.00	75 bu	$ 90.00
Corn	1.20	--	--	75 bu	90.00
Soybeans	2.70	22 bu	59.40	28 bu	75.60
Wheat	1.40	24 bu	33.60	28 bu	39.20
Hay	20.00	2 tons	40.00	3.5 tons	70.00
Total gross per rotation			$205.00		$364.96
Total gross per acre			$ 51.25		$ 72.96
Expenses per acre other than taxes			$ 35.00		$ 38.96
Net per acre before taxes			$ 16.25		$ 34.00
Market price per acre			$175.00		?

Indicated net return on Soil "A" $16.25 + $175.00 or 9.29%.

Indicated net return on Soil "B" $34.00 + 9.29% or $366.00 A.

As an example - Soil "A," a moderately productive soil, has been proven by a number of reliable sales to have a value of $175 per acre without improvements. In a very productive soil area "B" there are very few sales because the land is tightly held. The problem is to estimate the market value of soil "B."

This estimate can be made by estimating the rate of net return before taxes as indicated by the market on an investment of $175 per acre on soil "A" under typical management and capitalizing the net return before taxes of soil "B" by this rate of return.

Table 4 shows the calculation needed to estimate net return per acre for both soils showing the assumptions made in each case on an owner operated basis.

The net return in dollars before taxes is estimated for soil "A" at $16.25 per acre after deduction of expenses including labor and management. The net return before taxes on soil "B" is estimated at $34.00 per acre after allowing for higher expenses due to greater production. The expected yields of soil "B" were determined by a review of the soil survey report.

The rate of net return before taxes, as indicated by the market for soil "A" is found by dividing $16.25 by $175. This indicates that the market expects a rate of return before taxes of 9.29% on an investment in farm land in this area.

Capitalizing the net return of $34.00 per acre for soil "B" by 9.29% would indicate that soil "B" should be valued in the neighborhood of $366 per acre.

These are some uses made of soil surveys in Ohio assessment practice. We could probably make more effective use of them and would welcome your suggestions.

CHAPTER 15

SOIL SURVEYS AND URBAN DEVELOPMENT--AN EDU-CATIONAL APPROACH

Harry M. Galloway[1]

THE AUDIENCE FOR soils information is becoming broader each year. The big expansion of interest in the nature of soils derives from attempts to learn their suitabilities for urban uses, those not directly related to producing food, feed and timber products. On one hand, there is the need for individual landowners to know what uses soils are adapted for and what uses may be unsound. On the other hand, increased emphasis on planning for the growth of communities has spurred an interest in knowing soil qualities and the mode in which soils occur in the landscape. These facts are finding more and more use to undergird sound planning. Soil surveys have become a recognized tool for quickly assessing the quality of particular land areas for a number of potential uses.

This paper reports a developing Cooperative Extension educational program as conceived in Indiana to make the soil surveys useful in urban development. The illustrations used here are taken from our own experiences. Much of the thinking behind our program, however, has come from ideas shared with those in other states. While we know that much education has been carried on elsewhere, we have made no attempt to study other programs in detail or report them in this paper.

Soils affect land uses.

Both the rapid population growth in numbers and its increasing mobility have placed more people in situations where soil conditions directly affect them. This is especially true in rural-urban fringe areas where people are moving to enjoy some of the amenities of conntry living. A lack of appreciation for soil properties have resulted in costly mistakes by many users who attempt to exploit soils for unadapted uses. Many problems have

---

1. Agronomy Department, Purdue University, Lafayette, Ind.

arisen simply because people don't realize that soils have different values for different uses.

Sound uses of soils near growing cities and towns and around our recreational areas depend on a group of effective soil properties. Soil textures, permeability, variation in and arrangement of soil layers, types of soil clays, reaction and natural soil drainage are among the most important. These properties directly affect soil stability, strength features, corrosion potential and water transmission properties. Frost heave potential, soil bearing strength, drainability and shear strength are also affected by the soils properties and, in turn, these affect urban soil uses. Because soils are so different in these respects, they vary greatly in their suitability for building sites, parks, airports, use as borrow for highway subgrade and other uses.

People's soil knowledge varies greatly.

Because farmers are close to the land and work on, or dig into the soil at all times of the year, they are usually well aware that soils are quite different from place to place. Educational efforts by Cooperative Extension Service, Soil Conservation Service and other agencies have helped farmers understand soils. Soil maps, made in soil surveys, have become basic tools around which farmers lay their management plans.

Unlike the farmers, most urban people, do not have sufficient contact with the soil to develop an appreciation of how its features affect its uses. While many people depend upon the judgment of architects, engineers, and developers as they plan new projects, others do not seek sound advice. Some are misled by developers who do not know about adverse soil conditions or who consciously try to hide them. There is a wealth of knowledge uncovered by soil and geologic surveys which could help urban people with land use problems just as it has helped farmers. It is this wealth of survey data and reports that we are attempting to put to use in Indiana.

Making urban people soil-conscious.

A few years ago in Indiana, soils people began to strive for wider understanding of ways in which soils affect urban people and their programs. The need for this knowledge became apparent as the traditionally agriculture-oriented Extension Service broadened its concepts and moved into certain areas of community development. Through the county extension agents and Soil Conservation Service workers, we have begun to reach out to groups with whom we have not had normal contacts in the past. Contacts have been developed with state and county health workers, county planning commissions, the State Division of Community Planning, builders and developers associations, watershed sponsoring groups, highway departments and many public officials. We have showed them how soils differ and how soils maps can clearly locate these differences. Attempts have been made to teach some groups how to use soil maps. Special schools have been conducted for sanitarians, planning directors, builders and developers associations, real estate appraisers, tile drainage contractors and for the general public.

We have also tried to indicate what geologic and water information is available and of value to people for their particular purposes. Special schools to help county leaders understand soil and water resources as they affect community development have been held in about 20 counties.

Soil teaching programs.

The "awareness phase" to show how soils knowledge can be useful to individuals and groups across a broad spectrum of interests is well along in Indiana and in many other states. We approach an "action phase," such as we have had in many another program in Cooperative Extension through the years. This will involve not only getting soils maps and reports into use more effectively, but will also demand an agressive basic soil teaching program.

Many of the techniques for teaching urban soil uses have been borrowed from methods used in teaching farm people about soils. Monoliths (trays of natural soil sections to a 4-foot depth) and colored soil slides with brief simple labelling are proven devices for teaching soil characteristics and are useful for both farm and urban audiences in group meetings. Brief, concise and graphic soils descriptions explaining the points of interest about the soils are essential in discussing or writing about soils for local uses. Block diagrams, relating soils to parent material, topography, and location in the landscape, help people immeasurably. These aids have all been used for years with farm groups and are useful for both inside meetings and field trips with urban groups.

Visual methods of helping people understand soil geography have proven useful. These allow people to relate soils to localities where they live and help orient large groups in inside meetings. We also try to see that groups are carefully oriented before we take them on field trips. Soil association maps help accomplish both these objectives. Geologic background woven into the soils story always seems to heighten interest of urban as well as rural audiences.

Overhead projection of specially prepared, colored soil association maps is effective as it allows everyone to see the map areas readily. Local features can be handily indicated. If each soil association is related to locally known landmarks like highway intersections, schools, parks, quarries, lakes or streams, people relate soil areas with these landmarks. Establishing rapport with an audience early in the meeting can often be done this way and leads to heightened interest of each one attending. If something interesting can be recounted about one or two major soils in each association, the chances are that the audience will soon feel oriented. Each person will have some knowledge of soil properties in his own area.

We have learned much from teaching programs.

In teaching the layman to use soil maps, experience has shown that they are complicated, hard to orient to, and difficult to understand fully. Reports are lengthy, highly descriptive and not too well user-oriented. While we suspected this difficulty years ago, having to teach groups to use survey publications has made the fact very clear.

To teach a better understanding of using soil maps, laymen have been encouraged to work with them in meetings. A soil survey use exercise helps them learn how the survey map itself is useful and how use suitabilities can be assessed from the survey report. The version in current use calls for the determination of all map cultural symbols and asks the student to list each soil map symbol found on a quarter section assigned to him. He then finds the name of each soil and its capability and use limitations for farming. In another section he is asked to study the use possibilities of the same soils for seven urban purposes.

We have also learned that while soil characteristics affecting water movement, storage and soil drainage are of primary interest in the humid area, these are not usually well understood. Simple demonstrations and slide pictures have been developed to help people understand water movement principles. The principles are then related to soils of different nature common to the area under study. This is done with monoliths or colored slide pictures with appropriate labels.

Four simple, but effective, soil demonstrations which we have used successfully before groups are described in the appendix at the end of this paper.

Educational programs stimulate demands for new surveys and interpretations.

Partly as a result of this soils education program, the interest in soil surveys and interpretations for urban uses has boomed. Requests for surveys now far exceed the ability of our survey program to provide on a county by county basis. The requests are now being screened very carefully. Educational meetings in interested counties help explain the uses and values of soil surveys. Local officials are then asked to justify their needs for a survey to cooperating agencies. They are also being asked to help finance the survey due to added costs of the work in the urban areas.

In Indiana, as elsewhere, certain counties are being surveyed progressively, aiming at later publication. Scattered mapping is done in other counties to service the farm planning needs. To put these modern survey field sheets to more immediate and greater use to guide urban land development, interpretations are being developed early in the survey as field mapping progresses. This helps short-cut the long wait till soil reports are published.

Local people, representing potential soil survey user groups, form steering committees in progressive soil survey counties to help guide the surveys. These people help choose the areas where soil mapping is needed first. They are invited to the field occasionally to study typical soils and see how these are mapped. They help design a local publicity program on the uses and values of soil survey information as the survey moves along. It is they who usually demand that some type of report be made available to use with the field sheet maps as these are released. Sometimes a responsible local official purchases each field sheet map as prepared and aims toward a complete set of maps for local use. Steering committees are encouraged to raise money locally to reproduce a limited number of copies of a soil report to go with these field sheet maps. Such reports are called "interim soil survey reports." These furnish data from which the single-purpose colored suitability maps, so useful to local planning officials, can be drawn.

Interpretations assembled for "interim" reports are later used in the published soil survey report. Both "interim" and new published soil survey reports are taken to public meetings and

explained to representatives of various groups who would benefit
from knowing about soils in their work. Soil survey use exer-
cises are particularly helpful here.

Comprehensive planning spurs survey interest.

Greatest interest in using the soil surveys has come from
counties organizing planning commissions and beginning comprehensive planning. For example, Lake County, Indiana, employs a
soils scientist in the Cooperative Extension office to interpret
soil maps being made by the progressive soil survey. He works
closely with the consulting planners who are preparing a revised
county master plan. He also works with all persons or groups
needing special soils help. He carries on an aggressive education program which includes preparing soil maps and brochures
for cities which are looking toward their future growth and wish
to plan it better. More will be said about his program as this
symposium moves along.

New interpretations are being made available.

The urban ratings of soils depend upon engineering test data
and engineering soils classifications which have become a part of
published soil surveys only in the past 6 to 8 years. From these
test data engineering soil properties are estimated. A group of
such properties considered together determine how suitable a soil
may be for any one use. Another use suitability will be determined by a different group of properties. In order to organize
information for ready use and to keep urban suitability ratings
uniform, Soil Conservation Service has recently prepared charts
of soils interpretations for a number of purposes which include
the following tables to date:

1. Engineering test data for about 65 Indiana soils types. This
   sampling will continue until topsoils, subsoils and parent
   materials of all important Indiana soil series have been
   tested.
2. Estimated physical and chemical properties of Indiana soils.
   These have been assembled from actual test data where
   available and by relation to other soils of similar properties
   where tests were not available.
3. Interpretation of the soils of Indiana for rural and urban development. Includes limitations for several agricultural and
   urban types of land uses most frequently needed.

SOIL SURVEYS AND URBAN DEVELOPMENT   143

4. Interpretations of engineering properties of major soils in Indiana. Nonagricultural (urban).
5. Interpretations of engineering properties of major soils in Indiana for agriculture.
6. Interpretations of the soils of Indiana for 6 types of outdoor recreation.
7. Interpretations of soils of Indiana for wildlife habitat and kinds of wildlife.
8. Predicted yields for soils of Indiana under two levels of management.

All of these interpretations are prepared for limited use by technicians. They attempt to set out the limitations in terms of slight, moderate, severe and very severe for each potential type of use or for each important engineering property. Causative factors are given for each rating. The technician is expected to advise of soil limitations and not rate soils for use as good, fair, poor or unsuited. While it is not contemplated to release these tables for wide distribution, they will give background information for preparing brief "interim" reports covering soil areas such as around expanding cities or by townships or counties.

What lies ahead?

There are definite limitations to how much an urban soil teaching program can hope to accomplish! It will never replace the need for individual consultation with the soil scientist or soil engineer regarding specific projects. Rather, it should be re- garded as a training step toward making people conscious of how much soil properties do affect uses.

Planning commissions must constantly consider land use changes and must update the ordinances which regulate zoning. Soil information, packaged well for use and understanding, can become a regular working tool of such groups who may function very well without professional soils help. This will depend upon how well they are trained to understand the soils data initially.

Better methods of reaching select audiences of people not accustomed to dealing with Cooperative Extension and Soil Con- servation Service must be developed. More printed material about soils which can be distributed by agencies such as State and local health boards are planning commissions must be de- veloped. Soils training will be developed for many groups of employees who have regulatory or inspection functions so they can understand the soil principles and recommend more intelligently.

Magazine and newspaper articles will continue to call attention to soils problems and possible solutions.

In the future we may develop soil training in a number of outdoor laboratories in key urban areas. Soil pits could be dug in contrasting soils to illustrate a range of soil properties. Tours to train people with a range of interests could be organized when convenient. Visuals and data developed for soils at these laboratories could be used over and over again. The soil judging program for youth could make use of the soil pits. Conceivably, the soil judging program could be expanded to include children not enrolled in 4-H Clubs or FFA Chapters. Science teachers might use the same methods to expand interest in soils in science projects. These teachers could obtain help by studying soils at such laboratories. The 4-H soil and water conservation project, including the collection of soil micromonoliths, would be benefitted.

In the future, additional Extension personnel may be working in the larger urban centers to assist community development by interpreting soil surveys for these audiences. The methods of doing this are being pioneered at this time.

If this were to be rewritten 10 years hence, much more experience could be related. The methods of informing people may be different at that time. However, no matter how completely planning commissions, engineers and developers and others use soil facts to make better decisions, we can be sure of one thing: teaching simple fundamental facts about soils and how to use knowledge collected by soil surveys will still be high priority items in programs with the urban audiences of that time. Many more people will be available for these audiences. They will have needs much as urban people do today. The job is a very large one!

APPENDIX

Demonstrations that have been used successfully to relate principles of water movement in soils to the soils properties are listed as follows.

1. Soil percolation.

Glass columns filled with soils of the same texture but differing in degree of natural granulation and organic matter are placed near each other. Measured amounts of water are poured onto each column and time is kept. The audience observes the rate of percolation of water of the two soils in the columns and notes the gradual sealing of the less granulated soil, the increase in silt in the water, and the slowdown in percolation.

Discussion can relate these facts to the effects of grass on stabilizing structure, effect of texture on soil granule stability, use of mulches to prevent surface sealing, and increase in erodibility with puddling.

2. Soil limiting layers and water movement.

Two damp synthetic sponges with medium size pores are placed back to back and water is poured on top of one while they are held horizontally before an audience.   The amount of water which they absorb before it runs out the bottom is recorded.

Water is squeezed out of the sponges and a piece of blotter paper slightly larger than the sponges is placed on the top one with a lip extending over one end.   Measure the amount of water which the blotter and sponges will absorb when poured slowly over the blotter.   By slightly tipping the sponges toward the overhanging lip, water can be seen to run off the blotter end rather soon.   Compare the water absorbed with that absorbed by sponges alone.   Squeeze out the top sponge to see how little water actually penetrated the blotter.   The lower sponge will not have absorbed any.

The effects of pore size and water infiltration are discussed and the blotter is compared to a fine-pored, puddled surface area or a severely compacted one.

Repeat, but put the blotter between the sponges.   Water penetrates the top sponge quickly but little enters the lower sponge. Discuss the likeness of the blotter to the fine-pored condition of natural soil pans, plow pans, high clay layers or to severely compacted layers.   These occur under many gardens, lawns, playgrounds and athletic fields resulting from ill considered construction practices.

3. Hydraulic head and underground water movement.

The simplest illustration involves wetting one sponge held horizontally till water just begins to drip from the bottom.   Then turn it vertically and see that water quickly runs out the bottom.

Relate the vertical dimension (3 to 4 times the thickness of the sponge) to an increase in hydraulic head.   Explain how the same amount of water in a tall narrow vertical column has a greater "head" than when in a wide but shallow column.

A more sophisticated approach involves using soils of different textures in a system where water in funnels is connected by plastic tubing to other funnels containing the soils. The head is adjusted by raising the water-filled funnel so the water reservoir exerts pressure through the tubing to the soil in the other funnel. The time needed for the water to reach equilibrium in adjoining funnels is related to soil permeability which is related to soil texture, structure and porosity.

Discussion brings out how ponding around a foundation creates a hydraulic head. This creates greater pressures on basement walls and floors if soils are porous and sandy than if the soils are fine pored silts or clays.

4. Soil capillarity and water rise.

Small damp sponges of different pore size are stood on end in a shallow dish of colored water and the time is noted for the water to rise to their tops. If started early in a meeting, the fine-pored sponge may wet completely by the middle of the meeting, whereas the coarser one will not pull water as high.

Discussion relates the ultimate height of capillary rise from a water table to soils of different texture and pore size.

A system of water in a porous clay cup sealed to a mercury manometer will illustrate the suction forces exerted by dry soil for moisture. The water-filled cup, when placed in sieved silt loam soil, will give off water to the soil and exert a pull on the mercury reservoir causing mercury to rise in a capillary tube. When started early in a meeting, the mercury will rise 10 to 15 inches before the end and the wetting soil may be observed through the glass jar which holds it.

This demonstration shows that water moves from a moist zone to a dry zone with suction forces exceeding those of gravity. The idea can be applied to show how high water can be expected to rise from a water table reservoir and how the height of water rise depends on soil texture. The need for a vapor barrier in construction and the reason builders can plan basements in some soils and not in others are easier to understand after seeing this demonstration.

CHAPTER 16

EDUCATIONAL PROGRAMS TO AID AGRICULTURAL USERS OF SOIL SURVEY REPORTS[1]

O. W. Bidwell

EDUCATIONAL PROGRAMS to distribute soil survey reports have existed for some time. However, only since the late 1950's have they been used nationwide. The 1959 Saline County, Kansas, [1] soil survey educational meetings were not spectacular compared with later meetings, however, they demonstrated that farmers really wanted to learn more about the soils they farmed. Once they became aware that soil information was available, they made an effort to obtain it.

Now many states report similar experiences; some have had six or more years experience operating a successful soil survey education-distribution program. This article reports on successful programs and factors responsible for their success, based on answers to a questionnaire sent to the 50 States and Puerto Rico.

Questionnaire replies were received from 56 respondents representing the 51 political units. Thirty-six of the respondents (64%) were from Land-grant Colleges and Experiment Stations; 24 (43%) represented the Cooperative Extension Service. (Four were joint employees of the Extension Service and the Land-grant College and/or Experiment Station.) Ten (18%) of the Extension Service employees had the title of Extension Soil Conservationist.

Thirty-three states reported having soil survey distribution-education programs of some kind as of July 1, 1965. Ten additional states reported plans for such programs. Of the 33 states, 27 used community meetings as an important device to distribute soil survey reports. Six used leader-training meetings, and four used one countywide meeting.

Where community meetings were used, the number varied from 1 to 20. The consensus, however, was that at least three meetings per county were needed to provide all interested persons an opportunity to attend. Additional meetings, of course, brought out additional people. The number of meetings for counties with attendance exceeding 25% of the farms in the county is given in Table 1.

---

1. Contribution No. 945, Department of Agronomy, Kansas Agricultural Experiment Station, Manhattan.

147

Table 1. Counties for which community meeting attendance equaled or
exceeded 25% of the total number of farms.

County	State	Atten-dance	No. of meetings	Attendance per meeting	% of farms
Geary	Kansas	512	4	128	112*
Greeley	Kansas	183	2	91	67
Logan	Kansas	214	3	71	57
Wabash	Illinois	325	6	55	54
Clinton	Ohio	700-800	4	175-200	50-60
Adams	Iowa	550	10	55	50
Hamilton	Kansas	186	4	46	49
Brown	Kansas	650	5	130	46
Stanton	Kansas	106	2	53	43
Kearny	Kansas	130	5	26	42
Stevens	Kansas	150	1	150	38*
Kimball	Nebraska	160	3	53	36
Dundy	Nebraska	150	1	150	33
Shelby	Iowa	504	14	36	28
Monona	Iowa	400	20	20	27
Sargent	North Dakota	272	9	30	27
Morton	Kansas	76	3	25	26
Newton	Mississippi	200	1	200	25

* Counties having dinners to which women were invited and counted.

The 33 states distributed 176 soil survey reports through their distribution programs from January 1, 1960, to July 1, 1965, a period in which the Soil Conservation Service published 191 reports. Eight of the 33 states reported an excellent program; 24 reported a satisfactory program; and 1 said that its program was unsatisfactory.

Replies from the eight states were studied to determine factors responsible for the excellent programs. A summary of their replies is given in Table 2. In all eight states meetings were arranged jointly through the cooperation of the Soil Conservation Service, the Agricultural Experiment Station, and the Cooperative Extension Service, with the latter generally taking the leadership. All states reported that their successful meetings depended on good mass media support. All felt that women should attend the meetings, however, only Iowa, Nebraska, and Kansas made special efforts to welcome women.

As indicated above good publicity was recognized as one of the important factors in drawing a large attendance. News articles and radio and television appearances were used to publicize the meetings. In several states the chairman of the Soil and Water Conservation District Board of Supervisors and the chairman of the County Extension Council jointly sent invitations to all farmers and land owners in the county. Kansas publicized its county community meetings by bringing the State Conservationist, Extension Director, and Experiment Station Director in to talk to the county leaders at

Table 2. Factors responsible for successful soil survey programs as judged by individual states.

Meeting factors	Arkansas	California	Illinois	Iowa
Kind of program	Community meetings, clinic, announcements	Field tour and meetings	Community meetings, announcements	Community meetings, announcements
Preferred time	Winter	Fall or spring	Fall or spring	Fall and winter
Avg no./county	4	---	5	4-20
Surveys distr.	1	5	2	9
Yrs. operated	5	10	2/3	8
Preferred attendance length	20-30 2 hours	50-70 1½ hours	50-75 2 hours	35-60 1½ hours
Reasons for success	Agency cooperation	Interest in soils	Planning, publicity, program	Agency cooperation, planning
Drawing cards	Discuss survey reports at other meetings	Have farm advisors publicize	Program	Stress economic importance of report
Effective visual aids	Soil monoliths	Soil monoliths	Soil monoliths (scale models)	Survey reports, slides, charts
Suggestions for planning an educational program		Organize, publicize, good speakers, field trips	Generate enthusiasm in leaders and audience	Plan, publicize, cooperate

	Kansas	Nebraska	Oklahoma	Tennessee
Kind of program	Leader training and community meetings, field tours	Community meetings, announcements	Leader training and community meetings	Organizational and community meetings, field tours
Preferred time	Winter or spring	September to March	Varies with area	When farmers are free
Avg no./county	1-5	1-9	2-5	2-8
Surveys distr.	10	7	14	9
Yrs. operated	6	3½	6	6
Preferred attendance length	40-60 1½ hours	50-60 1½ hours	25-100 1½-5 hours*	12-15 ---
Reasons for success	Having farmers serve on committees	Publicity, hold reports until meetings	Planning, publicity, visual aids	Agency cooperation
Drawing cards	Free reports, refreshments	Free reports, refreshments	Free reports	Refreshments
Effective visual aids	Soil monoliths, report, colored maps	Monoliths, maps, slides, overlays	Slides, acetate overlays, field study	Soil maps, profile pictures
Suggestions for planning an educational program	Have many people help with meeting	Work with all agencies, use well-prepared materials	Have all agencies on program	Let county workers take reports to farmers

* Five hours needed when field trip is planned.

what they called a "VIP" (very important people of the county) meeting. Giving publicity to this event altered the county residents to the community meetings that soon followed.

Friendly community rivalry was used to increase attendance in Brown County, Kansas. Influential Illinois businessmen personally invited farmers to attend community meetings in that state. (Dakin[2] found that Kansas watersheds were organized more rapidly and more successfully when influential urban people were invited to participate in their organization.) Organized groups assisted in other ways. Boy Scouts in Geary County, Kansas, carried out demonstration experiments and assisted with a chicken barbecue at summer evening meetings. Logan County, Kansas, boy scouts delivered handbills. Future Farmers of America appeared on television (Figure 1) to publicize the Logan County meetings and assisted with refreshments in Kearny County, Kansas. Four-H members prepared posters to publicize Hamilton County, Kansas, meetings.

Distribution of the soil survey reports by Members of Congress prior to the meetings has been known to reduce meeting attendance. To eliminate this hazard several states have been able to delay congressional distribution until after the meetings, and in many cases, have prevented it completely, by explaining the educational program

Figure 1. Robert Brockelman, Vice-president of the Oakley FFA chapter appears on television to publicize Logan County, Kansas, Soil Survey community meetings. (Soil Conservation Service Photograph.)

to congressmen. Usually the congressman is happy to arrange to have his supply of reports distributed at the meetings. In Iowa, Oklahoma, and Kansas, Directors of Extension ask the congressman for their supply of reports when he is notified to place his order with the government printing office.

Finally, the most important element in the success or failure of community meetings was how well persons in the audience were trained to use the soil survey report. Programs to carry out this objective, of course, vary with different states, and with different counties within a state. Respondents agreed that the program should be altered to fit the community. Similarly, as revealed in Table 3, respondents showed remarkable concurrence in views regarding individuals who should participate in the meetings.

Table 3. Suggested speakers for the community meetings and the votes each received from these 8 states: Arkansas, California, Illinois, Iowa, Kansas, Nebraska, Oklahoma, and Tennessee.

County Agricultural Expension Agent.	8
Work Unit Conservationist.	8
Extension Agronomist, Soil Scientist and/or Soil Conservationist.	8
Soil Scientist (Party Chief).	7
Experiment Station Soil Survey Leader.	5
State Soil Scientist, Soil Cons. Service.	3
State Conservationist, SCS.	2
Chairman, Soil Conservation District.	1
Chariman, County Extension Council	1
Director, Extension Service.	1
Director, Experiment Station.	1

A soil survey educational program is to describe the soil survey report and explain its use. The most effective manner to accomplish those objectives based on experience of some 20 states, is through community educational meetings. For the meetings to be successful there should be a good program and large attendance. This is accomplished through: (1) joint planning by the cooperating agencies, (2) holding a number of meetings at the proper time, (3) obtaining good publicity, (4) using drawing cards, (5) having enthusiastic speakers who use good visual aids, and (6) obtaining the support of local people.

LITERATURE CITED

1. Bidwell, O. W. and Bohannon, R. A. Saline County, Kansas, promotes its soil survey. J. Soil and Water Conservation 15:121-123. 1960.
2. Dakin, R. E. Variations in power structures and organizing efficiency: A comparative study of four areas. Sociological Quarterly 3:228-250. 1962.

CHAPTER 17

QUANTITATIVE ASPECTS OF SOIL SURVEY INTERPRETATION IN APPRAISAL OF SOIL PRODUCTIVITY[1]

William R. Oschwald

CROP YIELDS are influenced by the properties of the soil where the crop is grown, the weather conditions that prevail during the growing season, the technology utilized in the production of the crop, and the ability of the crop producer to effectively combine the various factors into an efficient crop production system. In an industrial economy, such as the United States, inputs, such as commercial fertilizers, herbicides, large-capacity machinery, and others, may have greater influence on the crop production potential of a soil than do qualities such as natural soil fertility.

In appraising the productive capacity of the soils of an area, one needs to know the kinds and distributions of the soils, their input requirements, and expected responses to the input applications. A purpose of soil survey is to delineate areas of soils to aid in predicting the management or input needs and expected crop yields or outputs. The prediction of input needs and expected outputs requires knowledge of soil characteristics and the effects of the characteristics on response to applications of technology. The specificity of the predictions depends upon the homogeneity of the soil unit that serves as a basis for the predictions.

VERTICAL AND HORIZONTAL APPLICATION OF TECHNOLOGY

The degree of homogeneity of many present-day soil mapping units permits rather specific evaluation of the incremental effects of vertical application of technology. Riecken[3] has defined vertical technology as the appropriate yield-increasing inputs on a homogeneous soil situation. For example, for continuous corn, vertical technology would include the necessary inputs to provide for plant nutrition, water control, pest control, and other inputs regarded as

---

1. Journal Paper No. J-5318 of the Iowa Agricultural and Home Economics Experiment Station, Ames, Iowa. Project No. 1191 with Cooperative Extension Service.

essential components of a continuous-corn production system. Soil survey interpretations usually are based on the implicit assumption that vertical technology can be applied as needed to all areas of a soil-mapping unit. Interpretations based on this assumption define ₂ technologically possible level of production.

The degree of attainment of the technologically possible level is determined at least partially by spatial soil characteristics. These include size and shape of soil-mapping units and pattern of occurrence of associated soil-mapping units. Collectively, the spatial soil characteristics define the soil pattern of an area such as a field. The influence of soil pattern on crop production varies with the degree of mechanization utilized in the production system and is horizontal rather than vertical in nature. Horizontal application of technology determines the degree of attainment of the technologically possible level of production, i.e., the achievable level of production. An appraisal of soil productivity should include a consideration of horizontal as well as vertical aspects of the application of technology. The importance of vertical and horizontal application of technology in soil productivity appraisal can be illustrated through the use of a detailed soil map such as that shown in Figure 1.

The quarter section illustrated is in Adams County, Iowa, in the Shelby-Sharpsburg-Macksburg soil association area.[2] The soil pattern of this quarter section consists of (a) nearly level Macksburg (MaA) and gently sloping and sloping Sharpsburg soils (SaB, SaC2) derived from loess on the ridge tops, (b) sloping Clarinda (CcC) and moderately steep Adair soils (AcD2, ApD2) derived from paleosols on the side slopes below the loess soils, (c) moderately steep and steep, till-derived Shelby soils (ShD2, ShE2) below the loess soils and the paleosol derived soils, and (d) Colo-Gravity complex (CxB) in the stream valley and extending up the upland drains. This soil pattern includes soils that vary rather widely in input requirements and expected crop yields.

Soil productivity is frequently expressed in terms of crop yield per unit area. However, the crop production potential for a specific crop is a function of frequency of production as well as of yields per acre. Corn production potential may be expressed as bushels per acre per year as in Figure 2 to allow expression of both per-acre yields and frequency. These estimates are based on the assumption that the vertical technology for a high level of management can be applied as needed. The erosion control systems assumed would include terraces and a continuous-corn cropping sequence (CCCC) on the 2 to 5% Sharpsburg areas (more than 80 bushels per acre per year), terraces and a corn-corn-oats-meadow cropping sequence (CCOM) rotation on the 5 to 9% Sharpsburg area (40-60 bushels per

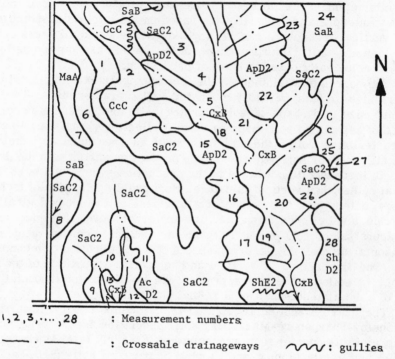

1,2,3,....,28   : Measurement numbers

———— · ————   : Crossable drainageways   ∿∿ : gullies

———— ·· ————   : Noncrossable drainageways

AcD2 : Adair clay loam, thin solum, 9 to 14% slopes, mod. eroded
ApD2 : Adair-Shelby complex, 9 to 14% slopes, moderately eroded
CcC : Clarinda silty clay loam, 5 to 9% slopes
CxB : Colo-Gravity complex, 2 to 5% slopes
MaA : Macksburg silty clay loam, 0 to 2% slopes
SaB : Sharpsburg silty clay loam, 2 to 5% slopes
SaC2 : Sharpsburg silty clay loam, 5 to 9% slopes, mod. eroded
ShD2 : Shelby loam, 9 to 14% slopes, moderately eroded
ShE2 : Shelby loam, 14 to 18% slopes, moderately eroded

Figure 1. Soil map of SW¼, Sec. 8, T73N, R32W, Adams County, Iowa.

acre per year), and contouring and corn, oats, and 2 or more years
of meadow (COMM) on the Clarinda, Adair, and Shelby areas (less
than 20 bushels per acre per year).

ANALYSIS AND SYNTHESIS IN SOIL SURVEY INTERPRETATION

The estimates of corn production potential are based on analysis of soil survey data, with respect to soil profile characteristics

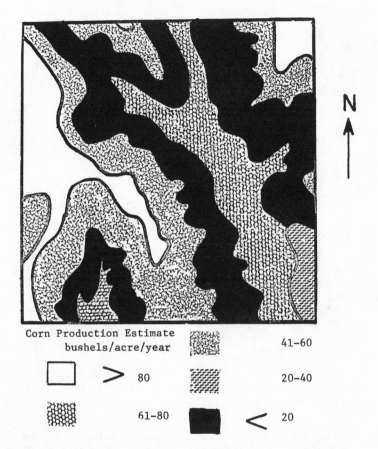

Figure 2. Corn production estimates: SW¼, Sec. 8, 173N, R32W, Adams County, Iowa.

and slope gradient, and <u>synthesis</u> of the soil survey data with pertinent data from other branches of soil science, crop science, etc.
The analysis phase literally involves "tearing apart" of a soil landscape as shown in Figure 3. This, a major function of soil surveys,
provides the most homogeneous soil area units consistent with scale
of mapping and the state of knowledge of soil science. In the modern soil survey report, however, interpretation with respect to appraisal of soil productivity essentially stops at the analysis phase
which includes the synthesis of pertinent "outside" data with the soil
survey data. If one were to approach the goal of "using each acre
according to its capability and need," Figure 3 would serve to delineate the various "parcels" requiring differential treatment. A
need in soil survey interpretation is to "in-gather" or "synthesize"

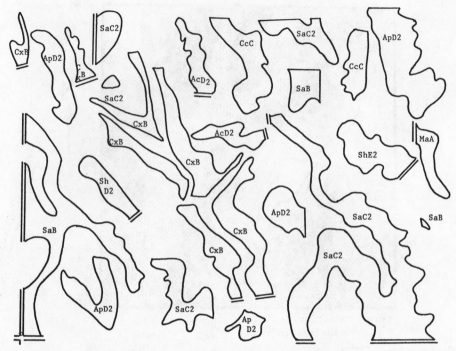

Figure 3. Soil map interpretation—analysis phase.

the component parts of a soil landscape into contiguous soil-use areas. Current methods of grouping soils for interpretive purposes do not effectively "in-gather" the component soils of a landscape.

The synthesis phase of soil map interpretation involves, not only the synthesis of response data, but also a synthesis of "in-gathering" of soil units into areas of various use potential. Figure 4 is an example of such a sunthesis. Size and shape of soil mapping units were taken into account in delineating the soil-use areas. The areas were subjected to the erosion control restrictions (maintain soil losses within soil loss tolerances) and additional restrictions of (a) equipment of 4-row capacity or larger would be used and (b) minimum area would be 10 acres, with sufficient regularity of shape to permit differential treatment and efficiency of machine operation. Compared with the potentials shown for vertical technology (Figure 2), corn production potential of Sharpsburg, 2 to 5% slopes, decreases from more than 80 bushels per acre per year to 41-60 bushels per acre per year and, for Colo-Gravity complex, from 61-80 bushels per acre per year to 20-40 or less than 20 bushels per acre per year.

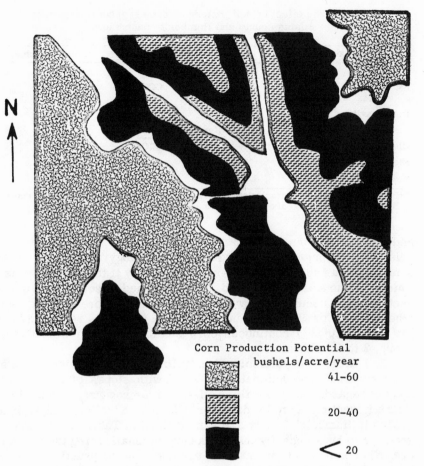

Corn Production Potential
bushels/acre/year

41-60

20-40

< 20

Figure 4. Soil map interpretation—synthesis phase.

SOIL PATTERNS AND CROPPING SEQUENCE SUITABILITY

The effect of soil patterns on cropping sequence suitability is illustrated in Table 1 for selected soil groups in a random sample of three quarter sections per township in each of the twelve townships of Adams County, Iowa.[2] Each of the 36 quarter sections in the sample were subjected to the erosion-control, equipment-size

---

2. Oschwald, W. R. 1965. The effect of size and shape of soil mapping unit in determining soil use potential. Ph.D. thesis. Iowa State University Library.

Table 1.   The effect of soil pattern on crop sequence suitability,
Adams county and Humboldt county, Iowa.

Soil group	Crop sequence*	Acreage suitable,† %
Adams County		
Sharpsburg, 2 to 5% slopes	CCCC	39.8
5 to 9% slopes	CCOM	53.6
Colo-Gravity, 2 to 5% slopes	CCCC	2.3
Humboldt County		
Clarion, 2 to 5% slopes	CCCC	53.6
Nicollet, 1 to 3% slopes	CCCC	74.6
Webster, 0 to 2% slopes	CCCC	87.5

* Based on soil profile characteristics and slope gradient. C=corn, O=oats, M=meadow.
† Based on consideration of soil patterns in a sample of 36 quarter sections.

and area limitations. The Sharpsburg group, 2 to 5% slopes, is suitable for continuous corn if vertical technology application is assumed, but has 40% continuous-corn suitability if the soil patterns in
which it occurs are considered. The combined effect of stream dis-
section and occurrence with predominantly more sloping soils
(Shelby soils on 9 to 14% and 14 to 18% slopes) is reflected in the
low (less than 3%) continuous corn suitability of the Colo-Gravity
group, 2 to 5% slopes.

Soil patterns of Humboldt County, Iowa, (in the Clarion-Nicollet-
Webster area) are dominated by soils with slopes of less than 6%
and are regarded as generally well-suited for row crop production.[2]
Quarter section sample data for Clarion, Nicollet, and Webster
groups in Humboldt County are summarized in Table 1. The Clarion
group, 2 to 5% slopes, frequently occurs in small, irregularly shaped
areas not suited for mechanical erosion-control practices. If soil
losses are to be maintained within present soil-loss tolerances (4
tons per acre per year), cropping sequences less intensive than continuous corn are necessary on about 50% of the Clarion group in the
sample. The pattern of occurrence with the less sloping Nicollet
and Webster groups results in some reduction in continuous-corn
suitability of areas of these soils also.

SUMMARY

Soil survey interpretation includes analysis and synthesis.[1]
Analysis includes the separation of a soil landscape into its component parts on a soil map and the determination of the profile characteristics of each of the component parts or mapping units. Analysis

of soil landscapes and of soil profiles is important in increasing understanding of a soil, its properties and genesis. Synthesis of this knowledge with information concerning the response of vertical technology is also important and will continue important in relation to soil resource use.

Analysis, in the form of a soil map, has served to "tear apart" the soils of a landscape or portion of a landscape such as a field or farm. In soil surveys, soils are separated on soil maps as different soil-mapping units, soil types, soil series and soil families. The soil user, however, uses a segment of space including a population of soils rather than the component parts individually. The user of soil survey interpretations may well question the usefulness of soil classification, as a basis for the application of technology in agriculture, if the interpretations are made for one soil-mapping unit without consideration of associated soil-mapping units.

The challenge for soil survey interpretation is to more adequately synthesize the component parts of soil landscapes into segments of space that are meaningful to the soil user in relation to the soil-use decisions he faces. Soil scientists as well as other scientists can make significant contributions in meeting this challenge. The degree to which the challenge is met will determine how nearly soil survey interpretation attains the objective of identifying soil-use alternatives to help people make more rational soil-use decisions.

LITERATURE CITED

1. Kellogg, C. E. 1961. Soil interpretation in the soil survey. USDA Soil Conservation Service.
2. Oschwald, W. R., F. F. Riecken, R. I. Dideriksen, W. H. Scholtes, and F. W. Schaller, 1965. Principal soils of Iowa—their formation and properties. Cooperative Extension Service, Iowa State University. Special Report 42.
3. Riecken, F. F. 1963. Some aspects of soil classification in farming. Soil Science 96:49-61.

CHAPTER 18

ROLE OF DETAILED SOIL SURVEYS IN PREPARATION AND EXPLANATION OF ZONING ORDINANCES[1]

M. T. Beatty and D. A. Yanggen[2]

ZONING IS ONE of several regulatory devices by which land-use plans can be implemented. Soil survey information has been used in subdivision regulations and sanitary codes as well as in the land-use planning process itself. Until recently it has not been used extensively in zoning. Our experience shows that detailed soil surveys are extremely useful in the development of zoning ordinances and in their explanation to local citizens. Our experience also shows that successful development of a zoning ordinance is a complex undertaking which must include, simultaneously, governmental activities and problem-oriented adult education. The role of soil surveys in each is described in detail, both with reference to a specific example county and to more general situations.

PHYSICAL BASIS FOR USE OF SOIL SURVEYS IN ZONING

Soil surveys are detailed, scientific inventories of all the major physical and chemical characteristics of soil. The soil characteristics studied in making a soil survey include sizes and arrangements of soil particles, kinds and amounts of minerals and organic matter, chemical reaction, slope, periodic or permanent wetness, and kinds and arrangements of horizons (layers). These characteristics interact to produce a response to any given land use. Published soil surveys include a text and maps which describe and show the locations of defined units with unique combinations of soil characteristics; from which, therefore, unique responses may be expected. Since soil is a major component of

---

1. Contribution from the University of Wisconsin, Madison.
2. Associate Professor, Soil Science Department and Wisconsin Geological and Natural History Survey, and Assistant Professor, Department of Agricultural Economics.

land, knowledge of the locations and responses of soils to various land uses can be invaluable in development of an ordinance. Its use allows land-use to be better fitted to the natural landscape and gives the ordinance stronger basis in fact than would otherwise be possible.

Examples of soil-related land use problems which reference to soil surveys may help to prevent are: building footing and foundation failures; wet basements; water erosion of farm fields, roads and gardens, malfunction of septic tank sewage disposal systems; flooding, etc.

LEGAL BASIS FOR USE OF SOIL SURVEYS IN ZONING

Since incorporating detailed soil surveys into a zoning ordinance is a new concept, the basic issue of its legal validity must be considered. This is a question that cannot be answered in the abstract. It will depend on a number of factors including: (1) the particular state's zoning enabling legislation, (2) judicial interpretations of these statutes, (3) specific uses made of the soil survey information in the ordinance, (4) administrative techniques used, and (5) the application of the ordinance to a particular fact situation.

Several general considerations are important. The use of soils information for zoning is compatible with the basic objectives of the Standard State Zoning Enabling Legislation on which many states present zoning enabling legislation is based. It can be particularly useful as an additional factual basis for the division of an area into districts for the purposes of regulating the use of land and the density of population.

The basic test of the zoning police power is its reasonableness. Reasonable use of soil survey information in zoning must be based upon a recognition of both its potentials and its limitations. Imaginative drafting techniques and administrative devices can be used to overcome many of these limitations.

EXAMPLE OF HOW SOIL SURVEY HAS BEEN USED

The development of a rural zoning ordinance for Buffalo County, Wisconsin (1965) illustrates, in part, the role soil survey can play in zoning. Figure 1 shows the sequence of steps in governmental activity (upper line) which were involved in development of the ordinance. The detailed soil survey of Buffalo County

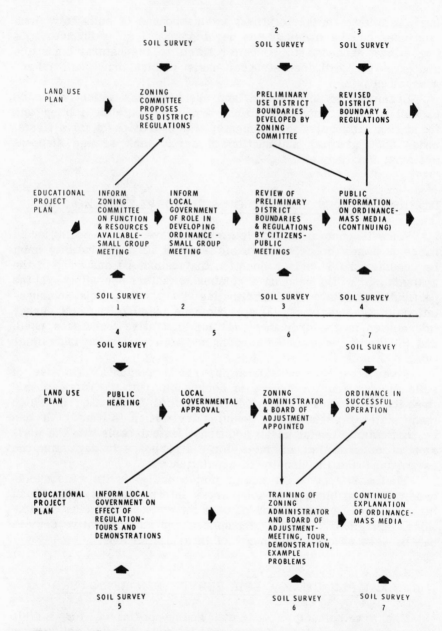

Figure 1. Suggested sequence of activities for development of a rural zoning ordinance.

by Thomas et al. (1962) is shown as an input to several of these steps. The way it was used is described to give an actual example of its role.

Work began with a survey of existing land use by a zoning committee of the county board of supervisors. The various uses in the unincorporated areas were identified and plotted on maps. The committee considered likely trends of future development and decided that farming would continue to be by far the most extensive land use; rural nonfarm homes and recreation would increase considerably, with commercial and industrial activities growing at a somewhat slower pace. The committee set up and developed regulations for six primary use districts (agricultural, residential, recreational, flood plain, commercial and industrial) to foster compatible groupings of the various land uses.

Then the soil mapping units from the detailed soil survey were combined into categories that were relevant to the development pattern the committee foresaw for rural land in the county (Step 1, Fig. 1). The major groups established were wet soils, steep soils, flood plain soils (all with special problems) and suitable soils (without special problems). Next, the major soil groups were compared to preliminary maps of primary zoning use districts to see if permitted uses could be located on soils with suitable characteristics (Step 3, Fig. 1).

Since this was not entirely possible the committee established supplementary or overlay districts. The ordinance provides that, if soils are not a special problem, the basic uses permitted are those established by the primary zoning use district. For areas with problem soils, these overlay districts provide additional controls. Some details of the overlay districts will illustrate their uses and the needs for their establishment.

Wet soils. Overflowing septic tank seepage fields and wet basements are problems in parts of Buffalo County. Soils which are wet because of periodic high ground water were identified and placed in a wet soils overlay district. Any use which requires a septic tank or a basement is prohibited unless special provisions are made to elevate them above the water table by filling the area with permeable soil. The applicant must submit results of percolation tests run on the fill after it is in place. Footing drains and sump pumps may also be required where necessary.

Steep soils. Much of the land in the county is steep. Bluffs contribute to the great scenic beauty of this area but pose special problems in building construction. There is danger of erosion, building slippage and lateral seepage of sewage effluent to the surface of slopes.

The committee recognized these problems and also wanted to preserve the scenic values of this rugged landscape. All soils with slopes of 12% or more are in a steep soils overlay district. A Board of Adjustment, appointed by the County Board of Supervisors, must approve plans of persons wishing to build on lots of less than 10 acres in this district. The Board may grant permission to build only if certain conditions are fulfilled. These conditions may include satisfactory provisions for stable foundation footings, control of erosion, safe disposal of sewage, safe road layouts and preservation of scenic beauty.

Suitable soils. The remaining soils in the county are suitable for most of the common land uses if a minimum number of simple precautions are observed. Soil properties, however, influence the size of septic tank seepage fields needed for safe disposal of sewage.

The zoning committee felt it is unlikely that people selling or buying building lots will run standard percolation tests and adjust lot sizes accordingly. Therefore, soils which had no major limitations were placed into a suitable soils overlay district with three broad sub-groups (sandy, medium textured, and clayey). Building lots on sandy soils can be smaller for equivalent uses which generate sewage than can those on medium textured or clayey soils because the sandy soils are more permeable. Under the ordinance, the minimum lot size for various use requiring on-site sewage disposal depends on whether they are located on sandy, medium textured or clayey soils.

Percolation tests are recommended for determining sizes of septic tank seepage fields, but the minimum lot sizes insure that each building lot will be large enough for such a seepage field and have room left over for a second field if needed later. The minimum residential lot sizes for each of these three groups of soils approximated those which would be called for under State Board of Health regulations if percolation tests were run before the lots were subdivided and sold for building purposes.

The flood plain district is an example of a primary use district which can be established where a soil-related problem occurs in large or contiguous geographic areas.

Flood plains were equated with alluvial soils and landscape positions since they usually lie several feet below adjacent stream terraces, and are usually separated from the terraces by a short, steep escarpment. The alluvial soils were combined into a primary use district with boundaries defined on the basis of units shown on the soil map.

The zoning committee considered three alternative kinds of regulations for the flood plain district and chose regulations which prohibit residences and most other land uses, but permit farming, water control facilities, recreation and wildlife habitat development. They also made provisions for the Board of Adjustment to make site by site review of special cases and allow certain uses of flood plains providing prescribed conditions are fulfilled. These conditions may include installation of fill, levees or dikes on certain places in the flood plain and proof that the proposed use will not materially obstruct the discharge of flood water.

Zoning base map. Use of the detailed soil map as the zoning base map is a key feature of the ordinance. The agricultural, residential, recreational, commercial and industrial districts are superimposed on the 1:20,000 soil map.

In many rural areas it is difficult to find a base map suitable for zoning purposes. The 1:20,000 detailed soil map has a larger scale than most maps available for rural areas. It shows roads and approximate section corners (if present). The photo mosaic base makes it easy to identify locations by physical landmarks. Superimposing the basic use districts on the soil maps focuses attention on the relation between soils and land use. This prevents errors that could arise where separate maps are used. The final result is a single map on which the zoning administrator and applicant for a permit can see locations of both districts and soils (Step 7, Fig. 1).

OTHER POSSIBLE USES IN ZONING

Soil surveys are potentially useful in zoning in many ways which were not appropriate in the Buffalo County situation just described. Several examples are cited below. In each, the soil survey can be very useful in land use planning which preceeds zoning, but can also be incorporated into the zoning ordinance to specifically implement land use policies. In all cases the soil survey will be most effective if used in conjunction with other available resource inventories such as surveys of water, topography, subsurface geologic materials, visual environmental qualities, land cover, etc.

The soil survey can be very helpful in defining and establishing exclusive farming districts. In this connection the soil survey can help to delineate areas which are particularly responsive to intensive farm management and from which high returns in produce or profits may be expected. Often such areas have soils

with few limitations for other land uses. It may also be possible
to use soil surveys to delineate soils which are responsive to
intensive farming but which have severe limitations for home-
sites, roads, factories, etc. Some wet soils fit this description.

Soil survey information can aid in delineation of conservancy
zoning districts. It can also provide valuable information for
such districts.

Soils are often closely related to underlying geologic materials.
This should make it possible to use soil surveys, in both planning
and zoning, as a means of delineating districts which modify these
geologic materials, as for example, by extraction of sand, gravel,
building stone, or peat. At present, districts for these land uses
are often tied closely to existing developments; whereas, long
term future development might be more advantageous at other
sites. If these sites are identified by use of soil surveys, intelligent land use planning and zoning is facilitated. The soil survey
is frequently the cheapest and most universally available means
of identifying these alternative sites.

Another possible use for soil surveys in zoning is in connection with geologic maps to delineate districts where land use
should be designed to facilitate ground water recharge. Maps of
bedrock geology can delineate general localities for such districts,
but soil surveys can complement them by showing areas where
infiltration and percolation of water to aquifers is likely to be
most rapid. Soil surveys offer another advantage for this purpose
since they are often made at larger scales than are geologic maps
and thus can be used to delineate district boundaries more precisely.

LIMITATIONS OF SOIL SURVEYS FOR ZONING

Wise use of soil surveys for zoning involves consideration of
their limitations. First, not all land use problems are related
to soil and most land use problems involve factors other than
soil. The planning process preceeding zoning should establish
these relationships. Solution of problems arising from the relationship between community development and the ability of natural
resources to support activities of man will require use of other
natural resource inventories in plan preparation and implementation.

The scale of soil survey maps, the intensity of investigations
and the range of conditions within map units may limit use of
soil surveys for zoning. The typical soil survey map scale of

1:20,000 is not large enough to show precise locations and dimensions of use district boundaries in highly developed areas. Large scale insert maps may be needed if soil maps are used as zoning base maps. Enlargement of photo mosaic maps can be made, but because the aerial photographs are usually not fully ratioed and rectified, horizontal ground control may be a problem. Some early detailed soil survey maps do not have a photo mosaic base. This would severely limit their use as a zoning base map.

Soil varies within any area shown as one body or unit on a soil map. Some of this variation is deliberately allowed by soil scientists, some is not. Map units are allowed to encompass a (generally narrow) range in soil conditions because it is obviously impossible to set up absolutely homogeneous units and show then on a map at a reasonable scale. The range in soil conditions within a map unit is almost always narrow enough so that all of the unit will respond in the same way to a given land use. In nearly every map unit there are also small areas called inclu-- sions with soil conditions other than those described for the map unit. Often, however, these included soils will respond to a given land use in the same way as will the dominant soil in the map unit.

A few units on a detailed soil map may have been set up to include a rather wide range in soil conditions - a range wide enough to allow different soil responses to a given land use. These mapping units often carry the designation of miscellaneous land type or of soil complex. Miscellaneous land types are often very steep, frequently flooded, or very shallow to bedrock. Soil complexes include two or more soils which occur in such an intricate pattern that it is not possible to map them separately on normal scale soil maps. Both of these kinds of map units must be used with great care in a zoning ordinance.

Site factors may influence how soil map units are used in zoning. For instance, an area of nearly level, well-drained soil which is located below steep bluffs and which receives overflow water may require different treatment in a zoning ordinance than will the same soil in the middle of a broad plain.

PREPARATIONS FOR USE OF SOIL SURVEYS IN ZONING

The first step in using a soil survey for zoning, as well as planning, should be an exchange of information between the planner and a person thoroughly familiar with the soil survey. They should discuss the following factors in considering the extent to which soils information can be used and the particular substantive and procedural provisions to be prepared.

1. The type and intensity of development expected in the area under consideration
2. The level of confidence that can be placed in the interpretations made about each unit on the soil map
3. The areal extent and degree of limitations posed by soil conditions
4. The types and number of land uses affected by the limitations
5. The difficulty of overcoming these limitations
6. Alternate uses of the soils under present limitations and with the limitations overcome
7. The amount of detailed on-site studies needed in conjunction with the various land uses and the availability of technicians to perform these studies
8. Whether the problem soils have geographic continuity or are of a small or scattered distribution
9. The feasibility of using other regulatory devices for dealing with the problem

ZONING TECHNIQUES FOR USING SOIL SURVEY INFORMATION

There are several general techniques for using soils information. While they are presented separately here, they could be used in the same ordinance to deal with different soil-related problems. There are also common elements within these techniques so that the difference between these devices may be one of degree rather than kind. These elements could be combined to devise new techniques. The particular method used will depend in large part on the factors just listed.

Creation of primary zoning districts based upon soils information. As used in this context a primary use district is one which has both its own specified list of permitted uses and is separately delineated from any other primary use district. Soils information can be used both to delineate a primary zoning district and to help designate the uses permitted within it. The flood plain district in the Buffalo County ordinance described previously is an example of a primary use district delineated by soil survey. A decision to create a primary zoning district to deal with a soil-related problem might be based upon a determination that (1) it is directly related to soil characteristics, (2) limitations

are severe and difficult to overcome, (3) a number of land uses
are affected, (4) the area has geographic continuity, and (5) zoning is the most feasible regulatory device for dealing with the
problem.

Creation of a soil overlay district. Another method for using
soil survey information in zoning is to create overlay districts.
This type of district does not have its own list of permitted uses
but is used only in combination with one of the other primary use
districts.   It is designed to provide supplementary controls over
land use in addition to those of the primary district, with certain
specified additions or exceptions.   It can be delineated by using
the soil survey map as the zoning base map and superimposing
the primary zoning districts on it.   If, for example, an area had
a moderate percentage of its soil which had periodically a high
ground water table, a wet soil overlay district could be created.
This district could permit as a matter of right any use permitted
by the primary zoning district which did not require a basement
(which would be periodically wet) or a subsoil sewage disposal
unit (which would fail to operate under certain conditions).   Any
use with a basement or septic tank would be made a special exception and the conditions attached to such uses specified.   The
decision to create a wet soil overlay district could be based upon
the following determinations: (1) land use problems are directly
related to soil characteristics, (2) the limitations posed are
moderate and can often be fairly easily overcome with proper
corrective action, (3) not all land uses are affected, (4) those
soil units by themselves do not have a high intrinsic value for
esthetic, wild life production or recreational uses, and (5) zoning
is a feasible device for dealing with this problem, although a
sanitary code also has a role to play.

Development of a special section of the ordinance dealing
with soils.   A proposed town zoning ordinance for an urbanizing
area in Wisconsin contains a special section on soil restrictions.
This provision is directed at soils unsuitable for septic tanks,
There are two categories of soil groupings; soils with very severe limitations and soils with severe limitations.   All soil absorption sewage disposal systems are prohibited in the very
severe limitations category but the applicant is permitted to present evidence contesting such finding after which the Plan Commissions may affirm, modify or withdraw its finding.   An applicant desiring to build a septic tank on these soils must meet the
following conditions: (1) additional on-site soil investigations including percolation tests are made, (2) a soil scientist or soil
engineer certifies that there is sufficient area suitable for the

system, (3) State Board of Health regulations are met, and (4) the Plan Commission determines that the system overcomes the limitations. This method is much like the overlay district technique except that the detailed soil survey information does not appear on the zoning base map.

NEED FOR ADMINISTRATIVE FLEXIBILITY

There are two main reasons administrative flexibility is needed in using soil survey information. First, the zoning restrictions may have been designed not to prohibit certain development but merely to insure that necessary corrective action is taken. Soil conditions can be modified by filling or draining, for example. The restrictions placed upon septic tanks or basements on certain soils may be designed merely to insure that they will function properly if installed. In this case, if the limitations were overcome, the proposed land use would be permitted. However, there is a need for follow through in the form of an administrative determination that the proper corrective action is taken. Second, the soil survey information may not be precise enough to permit an unqualified determination that the soil conditions are in fact as represented by the soil map and report. Again, using septic tank restrictions as an example, the applicant may propose locating his disposal system on the borderline between two soil mapping units. Since boundaries between mapping units are usually gradational rather than abrupt, he may in fact be locating it on a suitable rather than unsuitable soil. There can also be small unmapped inclusions of dissimilar soils within an area mapped as a single unit so that he could in certain cases actually be putting his septic tank on a suitable soil although the mapped unit shows only an unsuitable soil.

TECHNIQUES FOR ACHIEVING ADMINISTRATIVE FLEXIBILITY

Zoning as a regulatory device must steer a course between two sometimes apparently conflicting principles. On the one hand, the regulatory provisions must set forth rules sufficiently precise to forestall arbitrary decisions. On the other hand, these rules must bear a reasonable relationship to the physical environment. The draftsman of an ordinance which incorporates information from the detailed soil survey must recognize that the physical properties of soils in the real world of nature do not always correspond to the sharp demarcations he desires. Administrative flexibility can prevent regulations which are either artifically precise or arbitrarily vague so that the ordinance allows for those situations in which a final solution of a soil-related problem cannot be made in advance. In these cases, the ordinance should contain the following elements.

(1) An adequate statement of standards which are sufficiently precise to isolate the facts that have to be found. For example, if a wet area is to be filled and used for waste disposal, the ordinance should require that there be a designated number of percolation tests run in a specified manner to determine the percolation characteristics for septic tank purposes of the transported soil.

(2) A hearing procedure where the applicant has an opportunity to present contrary factual data. If the soil survey maps as a single unit an area with soils both suitable and unsuitable for a septic tank, the applicant must be allowed to prove that he is in fact locating the disposal field on a suitable soil. However, the burden of proof should be on the applicant to establish this fact.

(3) Availability of comprehensive fact finding to the agency making the administrative determination. For example, if the ordinance contains a steep soil district with erosion problems, technical personnel could be called upon to provide information as to whether the proposed site could be safely developed and what steps would be necessary to reduce dangers of erosion. The zoning permit could then be granted upon condition that these steps be taken. Such technical advice is often available from state and federal agencies or professional consultants. Soil and water conservation districts, for example, often have memoranda of understanding with one or more state and federal agencies for technical assistance in solving soil and water problems and the services of these personnel could be obtained through the district.

STRUCTURING THE ORDINANCE

Because the use of detailed soil survey information is a new element in zoning, the ways in which it is being used and the reasons for using it should be clearly set forth in the text of the ordinance. This will avoid misunderstandings when presenting it to the governing body and general public. It will also be a favorable factor if the ordinance is under scrutiny by the courts. An awareness of the problems presented by relationships between community development and natural resource capabilities will have been developed during the planning process. The zoning ordinance should be drafted to make as explicit as possible what the soil-related problems are, what policy determinations were made concerning them and how the particular regulatory provisions apply to these problems. Specific drafting provisions will depend upon the particular problems sought to be regulated, the zoning mechanisms selected and the administrative devices used. Consideration should be given to including the following points which are designed to clarify the role of the soil survey in the ordinance.

(1) Incorporate the detailed soil survey map and report by reference. If interpretations in addition to those contained in the report are being used these should also be incorporated by reference if possible, or at least made an explicit part of the underlying factual basis of the ordinance.

(2) State that the granting of a permit does not constitute a representation that the soil will necessarily be suitable for the particular use proposed.

(3) Describe the characteristics of the soils and the problems associated with them. This can be in the form of a finding of fact by the legislative body that, e.g., "All the following designated soils have periodic high water tables which can cause wet basements or seriously interfere with the operation of sub-soil sewage disposal facilities."

(4) Designate the specific soils by mapping unit name and map symbol in conjunction with the particular regulatory provisions that apply to them.

(5) Provide a policy statement by the legislative body describing the particular objectives sought. Such a statement together with an adequate statement of fact can help avoid the possible objection of an illegal delegation of power to the administrative fact finding body. It can also clarify the role that the soil information is called upon to play. For example, the soil survey may be used to delineate a wetlands conservancy district which prohibits erection of most types of structures. This district may prohibit filling, draining, dredging and other activities which would extensively alter existing soil conditions. It should be made clear, if such be the case, that the unsuitability of existing soil conditions for the prohibited development is only one of several considerations. The major objectives may be to preserve these areas because they are water storage areas, fish and wildlife production grounds and objects of esthetic appreciation.

ROLE OF SOIL SURVEY IN EDUCATION

Public acceptance of a zoning ordinance is essential to its successful adoption and administration. Problem-oriented adult education can hasten this acceptance. There are three principal values that soil survey information can add to the educational aspects of zoning. First, it can relate a relative unknown (zoning) to a known (soil information) in the minds of local people. Second, it is an excellent source of illustrative and demonstrational material. Third, it can help to involve people from local groups such as soil and water conservation districts, local watershed organizations, irrigation districts, etc. and local resource technicians in the development and administration of the zoning ordinance.

After people are willing to develop an ordinance, the soil survey can be of real value in educational activities. Figure 1 (lower line) shows several points of involvement for soil surveys in a sequence of educational activities designed to accompany governmental action in development of an ordinance for Buffalo County, Wisconsin. In each case the use was tailored to fit the audience. Similar educational activities which involve soil survey would be needed in development of ordinances elsewhere. In step 1 the zoning committee was given detailed information about the soil survey and possible uses and limitations it had for zoning at a series of committee meetings. This was done by studying the application of various alternative regulations to land areas which the committee members were personally familiar with and had identified on the soil map sheets. The same thing was done in step 6 with the zoning administrator and the board of adjustment. The County Board (step 5) received similar but less intensive training.

The soil survey played a vital role in the educational meetings held as step 4 of the project. At these large meetings, which were held in each town of the county, there was not an opportunity for each participant to become thoroughly familiar with the soil survey report. Instead, the important soil conditions which it mapped were illustrated by slides, monoliths and diagrams and were discussed in relation to land use problems. Slides of flooded homes on alluvial soils, overflowing septic tanks filter fields on wet soils and roadbank erosion on steep soils were featured. The role of the proposed ordinance in controlling these and other soil-related land use problems was then described. This approach made sense to local citizens and they gained confidence in the proposed regulations quickly. These meetings were very important to the successful development of the ordinance. They gave people a chance to react to the ordinance before it was completed and to suggest changes they wanted to see incorporated into it. The relationship between soils and land use problems was also featured in the mass media used in steps 3 and 7 of the project.

Creativity is needed to develop a relevant plan for educational phases of zoning and to incorporate soil survey information into this plan in ways that will be most effective. The sequence of activities may need to be very different than that shown in Figure 1, but the goal should be the same: to inform government officials and local citizens of land use problems, of the role of zoning in implementing a land use plan, and of the role soil surveys have in developing a good workable ordinance.

LITERATURE CITED

Buffalo County Zoning Committee. Buffalo County Zoning Ordinance, 1965, Court House, Alma, Wisconsin.
Thomas, D. D. et al. Soil Survey Buffalo County, Wisconsin, U.S.D.A., Soil Conservation Service in cooperation with University of Wisconsin, Series 1957, No. 13.

CHAPTER 19

CHANGES IN THE NEED AND USE OF SOILS INFORMATION[1]

S. S. Obenshain[2]

THE GENERAL SUBJECT of this symposium is not a new one. When the writer came into the field of soil survey over 30 years ago, there was considerable interest in this subject. The Highway Department of Michigan was already employing men with soil survey experience to assist in planning highway construction. Kellogg and others were making soil surveys in North Dakota for use in tax assessments as reported in USDA Technical Bulletin No. 467. Land classification was also having its day with soil survey serving as useful background information. Even earlier, C. F. Marbut, head of soil survey of the old Bureau of Soils, cooperated with the Bureau of Public Roads in attempting to correlate road failures with types of soil.

Today the use of soil survey in land use planning is a subject of renewed and increased interest and thus deserves the attention it is getting at this symposium. It is the subject of three half-day sessions plus a number of papers on other programs. Certainly, it is important that those working in this field exchange experiences and ideas.

As an introduction to this symposium, a brief review of the recent developments in Virginia's soil survey program and its urban uses will be given. The extensive use of soil survey information in urban development began in Fairfax County, Virginia. A consultant firm, which was preparing a proposed land use map for the county, requested a detailed soil survey to be used as a basis for its report. Since Fairfax County had been previously surveyed, the cooperating agencies felt that the county should bear a substantial part of the cost of the field work for a more detailed survey. The county agreed to contribute some $30,000 toward its cost. The field work began in 1953 and was completed in 1955.

To protect the interests of Fairfax County, the Board of Supervisors appointed a soil survey committee which had the responsibility of not only seeing that the county's needs were met in the making of the survey but also that the agencies of the county government

---

1. Contribution from the Virginia Agricultural Experiment Station, Virginia Polytechnic Institute, Blacksburg, Virginia.
2. Professor of Agronomy (Soils).

were making the best use of the information as it became available. This committee, with the cooperation of the survey party, was largely responsible for the development of many new uses of soils information as the survey progressed. At the completion of the survey, the local committee appeared before the County Board of Supervisors and requested the appropriation of money for the employment of a soil scientist to advise the county governmental agencies in the use of the newly acquired soils information. After considerable discussion, and with the backing of a number of interested organizations, money was appropriated and the Department of Agronomy at Virginia Polytechnic Institute was asked to furnish a man qualified to act as the county soil consultant. In answer to this request, a senior field man from the VPI staff was assigned to this position and the college was reimbursed for his services. Approximately two years alter, this consultant resigned to become the first soil scientist employed by the Federal Housing Administration. He was replaced by another member of the VPI staff who had a similar background of training and experience in soil survey. After serving the county in this capacity for about two years, he was transferred to the county staff. Thus, Fairfax became the first county to hire a full time soil scientist.

A few months after the soil survey field work was completed, a preliminary report describing each of the soil units mapped, with a discussion of their suitability for urban and agricultural use, was published. The field sheets were enlarged to a scale of 1 inch = 400 feet, this being the standard scale for other maps of the county. These enlargements were on transparencies so that they could be readily reproduced for any user. Reproductions were kept available so that anyone could secure immediately a copy of a map giving the soil pattern on any parcel of land within the county. Attached to the map were mimeographed sheets describing each soil found in the area covered by the map.

The county soil scientist was busy answering calls from a limited number of departments from the beginning. With the passage of time, the number of requests has greatly increased. The 1965 annual report for Fairfax County shows that the soil scientist answered 3,257 calls during the year. While these requests covered 38 different items, the most numerous were: (1) checking soils for new septic tank disposal systems, 509; (2) furnishing detailed soil reports and maps for rezoning cases for Planning Commission and Board of Zoning Appeals, 88; (3) determining flood plain limits, 86; (4) determining trees and shrubs best suited to soils on property for screening commercial and industrial sites, 70; (5) information on depth to, and type of, hard rock, 63; (6) stabilization of steep slopes and soil slippage problems, 54; and (7) new school sites, 39.

In March 1958, Prince William County, which is adjacent to Fairfax County, appropriated money for its part toward the cost of a survey, and a party of Virginia Agricultural Experiment Station employees moved in. Field work in this county was essentially completed in 1961 and the man who had been in charge of the mapping remained in the county to assist in the interpretation of soils information. He is on the VPI agronomy staff and the county reimburses the college for this service. There are various reasons for the soil consultant remaining on the college staff. First, it insures that he remains a soil scientist, and second, he is relieved of local political pressure which might easily result if he were a local county employee. The county executive officer expressed the idea that it would be easier to convince his Board of Supervisors that the soil scientist should remain on the college staff if the college were bearing a portion of the cost. After considerable discussion with directors of the Agricultural Experiment Station and Extension Service, the Dean of the College of Agriculture at VPI, a policy was developed which commits the college to a financial participation. At present, the college is paying 1/3 of the salary for the county consultant. The county reimburses the college for the other 2/3 and bears the operating expenses. The consultant has a joint college appointment, 1/2 time Experiment Station and 1/2 Extension Service. Similar arrangements have been worked out with two other counties.

The Virginia soil survey program has, from the beginning, been a cooperative undertaking between the Agronomy Department of the Virginia Agricultural Experiment Station and a federal agency, now the Soil Conservation Service. At the present time, each field mapping party is composed of either Experiment Station employees or Soil Conservation Service employees. All other phases of the work are carried on cooperatively, beginning with an educational program where a county has indicated interest in a soil survey, through the publication of soil survey reports and follow-up work. Each county participates in the cost of its soil survey, which amounts to 1/4 to 1/2 of the cost of the field work.

Henrico County appropriated its part of the cost and a Soil Conservation Service party moved in to begin a soil survey about June 1, 1961. This was followed by a soil survey party of Virginia Agricultural Experiment Station employees in Chesterfield County. These two counties are in the Richmond metropolitan area. Soil surveys were then started in Stafford and Spotsylvania Counties, adjacent to Fredericksburg, with a Soil Conservation Service party in the former and a Virginia Agricultural Experiment Station party in the latter. Other counties with urban problems have already

committed their part of the cost of a soil survey, awaiting the time
when personnel will be available to start the surveys.

While it has been the policy in Virginia to require a detailed
soil survey as the basis of the county consultant's work, the surveyors have been forced into consultant work in two counties before
the survey was completed. One of these counties is being mapped
by a Soil Conservation Service party and the other by an Experiment
Station party. These problems have been taken care of in a slightly
different manner. In the county where the soil Conservation Service
party is mapping, the party chief is doing the consultant work and
the county has been willing to extend its financial assistance from
year to year. In the county where the Experiment Station party is
making the survey, the county, in cooperation with the State Health
Department, has agreed to reimburse the college for a soil consultant on the basis described above, who will work in cooperation with
the field party until the survey has been completed. The soil consultant will be seriously handicapped, however, until the survey has
been completed.

Making a major contribution to the wide use of soils information
in land use planning, is the cooperative program between the Virginia Polytechnic Institute and the State Health Department. Following the wide use of soils information by certain county public health
directors, leaders in the State Health Department proposed a cooperative program with VPI directed towards a study of the use of
soils information in a state health program. The Experiment Station assigned one of the men on the soil survey staff to work with
the State Health Department in order to pursue this study. At this
time, both the Agronomy Department and the State Health Department feel that this work has been highly successful and it continues
to grow. The Virginia Health Bulletin for December 1963-January
1964 describes many features of this cooperative program.

A soils course taught in the field during the summer for the
past nine years has also been a big factor in spreading the use of
soils information. This course was designed primarily for professional workers and was taught in the area where the participants
were working. The students spend most of their time in the field
learning how to interpret soil clues and to evaluate them for both
urban and agricultural use.

It is agreed that the task of working soils information into the
actual operational structure of local government is a selling job.
The use to be made of the information does, however, affect the
mapping and the correlary information secured. Both the mapping
legend and amount of detail mapped, in a county where urban
development is pressing, were altered with some bias on the urban

side. In making field delineations, the soil scientist is faced with the fact that the map he is making may be used as a guide with respect to whether the owner can sell his land for a housing development, for a shopping center, or for agricultural purposes. The amount of detail needed in areas of rapid urban development may affect the rate of mapping. The present rate of mapping in Virginia is from 1/4 to 1/2 square mile per day. The surveyor must constantly bear in mind that the program of use of soils information in urban development has succeeded due to the fact that the detailed maps and corollary information have saved the tax payers millions of dollars.

It has long been recognized that, to be effective, soils information must be presented in terms that the user can understand. Certain information not considered necessary in advising on the best agricultural use of soils may be quite significant as a basis for planning urban developments. All soils mapped in a soil survey are routinely analyzed for properties necessary in advising on agricultural use and management. In addition, soil mechanics determinations, formerly run by the Bureau of Public Roads, are now being made. These determinations include Atterberg constants, shrink-swell ratios, California bearing ratios, and moisture density curves. In some of the counties, the soil consultant is associated with the soil mechanics laboratory and runs determinations on as many of the soils of the county as possible. This has been of particular value in dealing with engineers. Measurements of water tables of different soils in relation to rainfall are being made, strengthening the cooperative work with the State Health Department. Percolation tests made with the health departments have given very useful information and have resulted in the re-evaluation of many soils relative to their suitability for absorption fields for individual sewage disposal systems.

The success in this new development is largely due to the results of the program. Virginia's program is primarily concerned with the detailed use of soils information as it applies to a particular spot or small area of land. For such an application, it is imperative first, to have a high quality detailed soil map and second, an experienced, highly competent soil scientist to fill the position of consultant. In other words, an experienced soil surveyor can evaluate the properties of the soils more completely than can be done by all the soil laboratory determinations now known. The initial success of the urban soils program in Virginia was due to the fact that at the time of its inauguration three very competent men, each with over 20 years of field experience, were on the college soil survey staff. These men set the pattern of the program as it developed. A necessary background for a county soil consultant is experience in soil mapping and evaluation.

POOR LAND USE

GOOD LAND USE

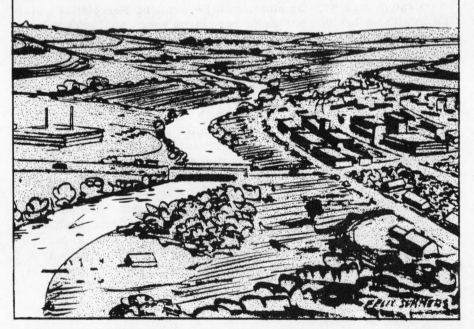

TALE OF TWO CITIES

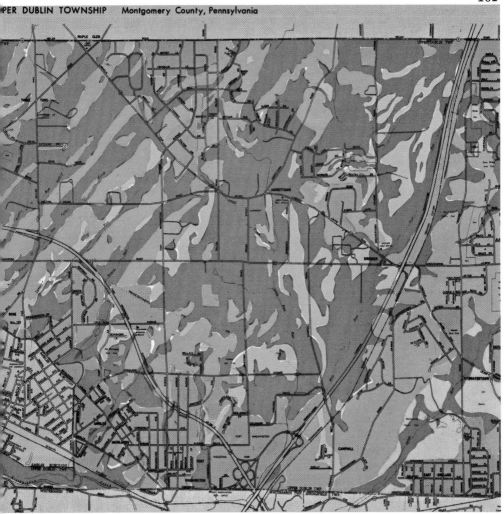

OIL CAPABILITY FOR ON-SITE SEWAGE DISPOSAL

Satisfactory

Satisfactory, But With Caution

Variable

Unsatisfactory

Made Land

0 400 800   1600   2400   3200   4000 Feet

Prepared by the Montgomery County Planning Commission
Court House, Norristown, Pennsylvania. December, 1964

0   ¼   ½ Mile

The preparation of this map was financed in part through an urban planning grant from the Housing and Home Finance Agency, under the provisions of Section 701 of the Housing Act of 1954, as amended, administered by the Bureau of Community Development, Pennsylvania Department of Commerce.

Source: Soil Survey of Montgomery County By Soil Conservation Service
of the U.S. Department of Agriculture 1960-63

Plate 1.   Soil capability for on-site sewage disposal.   (See p. 21)

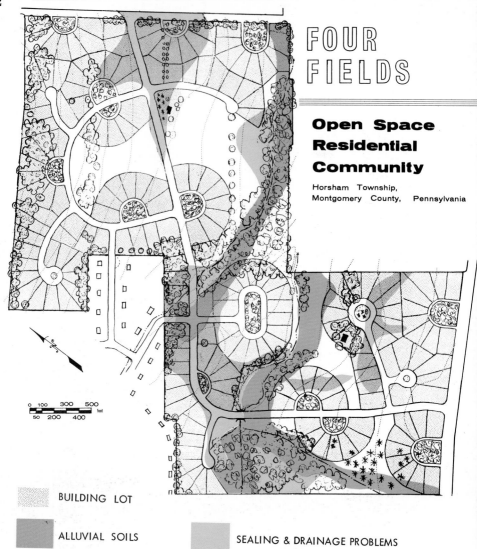

FOUR
FIELDS

**Open Space
Residential
Community**

Horsham Township,
Montgomery County, Pennsylvania

0 100 300 500
50 200 400 feet

BUILDING LOT

ALLUVIAL SOILS

SEALING & DRAINAGE PROBLEMS

Plate 2. Open space residential community, Horsham Township, Montgomer
Co., Pa. (See p. 23)

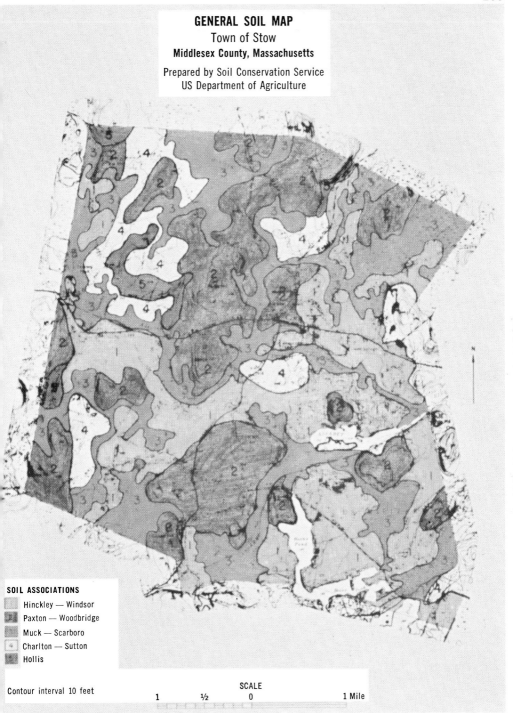

GENERAL SOIL MAP
Town of Stow
Middlesex County, Massachusetts
Prepared by Soil Conservation Service
US Department of Agriculture

SOIL ASSOCIATIONS
Hinckley — Windsor
Paxton — Woodbridge
Muck — Scarboro
Charlton — Sutton
Hollis

Contour interval 10 feet

SCALE
1   ½   0   1 Mile

Plate 3.   General soil map, Town of Stow, Massachusetts.   (See p. 62)

184

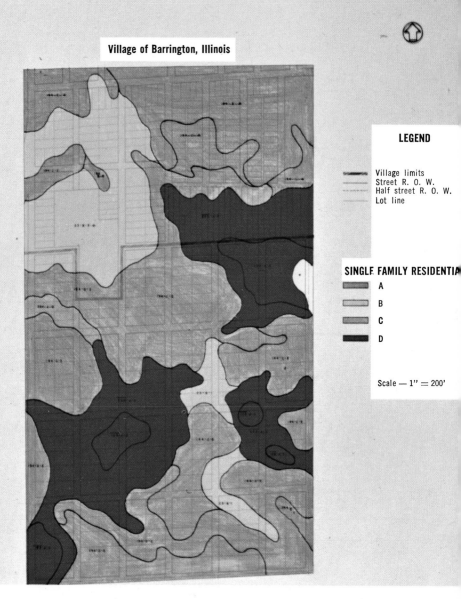

Plate 4. Grove Street subdivision soil map with project capability interpretation. (See p. 78)

A. Suitable with sewers
B. Suitable with sewers and foundation drainage
C. Suitable with sewers, foundation drainage and improved surface drainage
D. Unsuitable because of flooding, bearing capacity, water table, corrosion, shrink-swell, and percolation

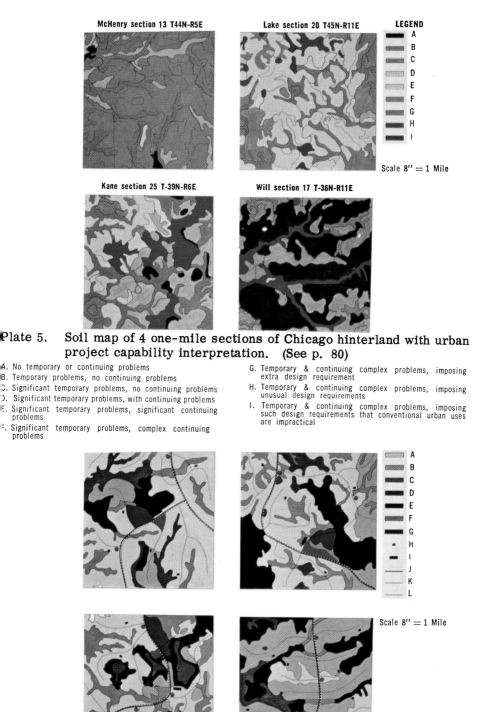

McHenry section 13 T44N-R5E

Lake section 20 T45N-R11E

LEGEND
A
B
C
D
E
F
G
H
I

Scale 8" = 1 Mile

Kane section 25 T-39N-R6E

Will section 17 T-36N-R11E

Plate 5. Soil map of 4 one-mile sections of Chicago hinterland with urban project capability interpretation. (See p. 80)

A. No temporary or continuing problems
B. Temporary problems, no continuing problems
C. Significant temporary problems, no continuing problems
D. Significant temporary problems, with continuing problems
E. Significant temporary problems, significant continuing problems
F. Significant temporary problems, complex continuing problems

G. Temporary & continuing complex problems, imposing extra design requirement
H. Temporary & continuing complex problems, imposing unusual design requirements
I. Temporary & continuing complex problems, imposing such design requirements that conventional urban uses are impractical

A
B
C
D
E
F
G
H
I
J
K
L

Scale 8" = 1 Mile

Plate 6. Preliminary urban development scheme based on soil capabilities. (See p. 81)

. Low density Residental
. High density Residental
. Commercial
. Industrial

E. Public parks
F. Private open space
G. Water
H. Grade school

I. High school
J. Through road
K. Collection road
L. Rapid transit

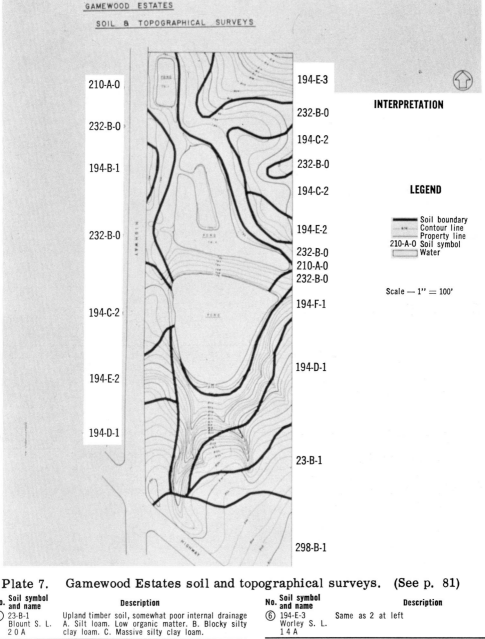

GAMEWOOD ESTATES

SOIL & TOPOGRAPHICAL SURVEYS

210-A-O

232-B-0

194-B-1

232-B-0

194-C-2

194-E-2

194-D-1

194-E-3

232-B-0

194-C-2

232-B-0

194-C-2

194-E-2

232-B-0
210-A-0
232-B-0

194-F-1

194-D-1

23-B-1

298-B-1

INTERPRETATION

LEGEND

Soil boundary
Contour line
Property line
210-A-O Soil symbol
Water

Scale — 1″ = 100′

Plate 7.   Gamewood Estates soil and topographical surveys.   (See p. 81)

(See p. 81)

No.	Soil symbol and name	Description
①	23-B-1 Blount S. L. 2 0 A	Upland timber soil, somewhat poor internal drainage A. Silt loam. Low organic matter. B. Blocky silty clay loam. C. Massive silty clay loam.
②	194-B-1 Worley S. L. 0 4 A	Upland timber soil, moderately good internal drainage. A. Silt loam. Low organic matter. B. Blocky silty clay loam. C. Massive silty clay loam.
③	194-C-2 Worley S. L. 1 8 A	Same as 2 above
④	194-D-1 Worley S. L. 2 8 A	Same as 2 above
⑤	194-E-2 Worley S. L. 0 4 A	Same as 2 above

No.	Soil symbol and name	Description
⑥	194-E-3 Worley S. L. 1 4 A	Same as 2 at left
⑦	194-F-1 Worley S. L.	Same as 2 at left
⑧	A-10-A-O Lena Muck 1 0 4 A	Depressional organic soil, very poor internal d age. Granular muck surface. Structureless r subsurface.
⑨	232-B-0 Ashkum S. C. L. 5 6 A	Low dark soil, poor internal drainage. A. clay loam — High organic matter. B. Blocky clay loam. C. Massive silty clay loam.
⑩	298-B-1 Beecher S. L. 5 8 A	Moderately dark upland soil, somewhat poor ternal drainage. A. Silty clay. Moderately high ganic matter. B. Blocky silty clay loam. C. sive silty clay loam.

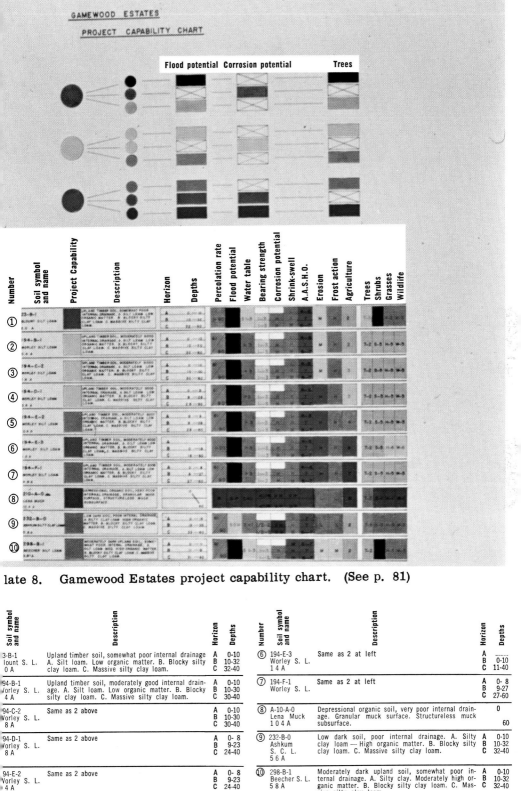

GAMEWOOD ESTATES

PROJECT CAPABILITY CHART

	Flood potential	Corrosion potential		Trees

Plate 8.   Gamewood Estates project capability chart.   (See p. 81)

Number	Soil symbol and name	Description	Horizon	Depths
3-B-1 Mount S. L. 0 A	Upland timber soil, somewhat poor internal drainage. A. Silt loam. Low organic matter. B. Blocky silty clay loam. C. Massive silty clay loam.	A B C	0-10 10-32 32-40
94-B-1 Worley S. L. 4 A	Upland timber soil, moderately good internal drainage. A. Silt loam. Low organic matter. B. Blocky silty clay loam. C. Massive silty clay loam.	A B C	0-10 10-30 30-40
94-C-2 Worley S. L. 8 A	Same as 2 above	A B C	0-10 10-30 30-40
94-D-1 Worley S. L. 8 A	Same as 2 above	A B C	0- 8 9-23 24-40
94-E-2 Worley S. L. 4 A	Same as 2 above	A B C	0- 8 9-23 24-40

Number	Soil symbol and name	Description	Horizon	Depths
⑥ 194-E-3 Worley S. L. 1 4 A	Same as 2 at left	A B C	0-10 11-40
⑦ 194-F-1 Worley S. L.	Same as 2 at left	A B C	9-27 27-60
⑧ A-10-A-0 Lena Muck 1 0 4 A	Depressional organic soil, very poor internal drainage. Granular muck surface. Structureless muck subsurface.	0 60	
⑨ 232-B-0 Ashkum S. C. L. 5 6 A	Low dark soil, poor internal drainage. A. Silty clay loam — High organic matter. B. Blocky silty clay loam. C. Massive silty clay loam.	A B C	0-10 10-32 32-40
⑩ 298-B-1 Beecher S. L. 5 8 A	Moderately dark upland soil, somewhat poor internal drainage. A. Silty clay. Moderately high organic matter. B. Blocky silty clay loam. C. Massive silty clay loam.	A B C	0-10 10-32 32-40

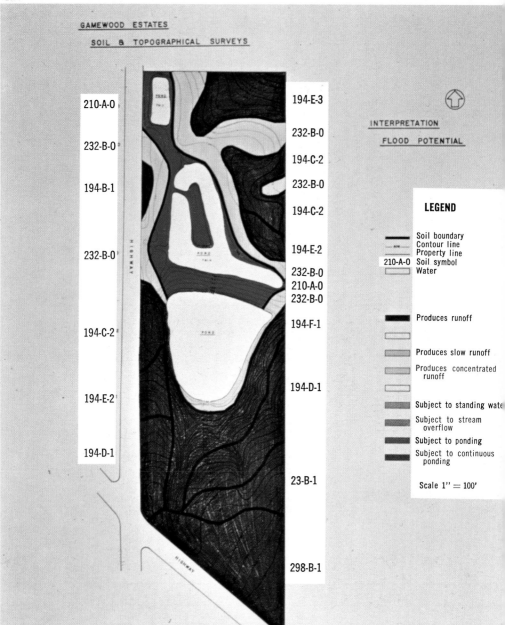

Plate 9.   Gamewood Estates soil and topographical surveys.   Interpretation-
flood potential.

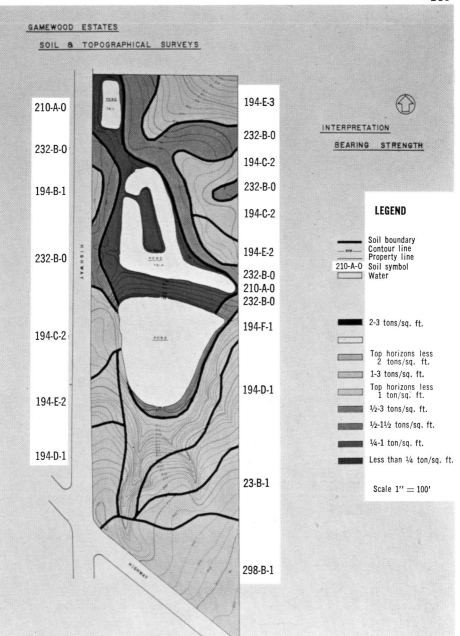

Plate 10. Gamewood Estates soil and topographical surveys. Interpretation-bearing strength.

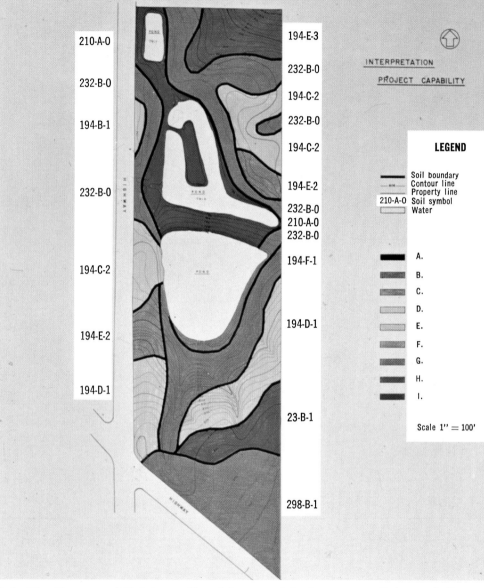

GAMEWOOD ESTATES

SOIL & TOPOGRAPHICAL SURVEYS

210-A-0

232-B-0

194-B-1

232-B-0

194-C-2

194-E-2

194-D-1

194-E-3

232-B-0

194-C-2

232-B-0

194-C-2

194-E-2

232-B-0
210-A-0
232-B-0

194-F-1

194-D-1

23-B-1

298-B-1

INTERPRETATION

PROJECT CAPABILITY

LEGEND

▬▬▬	Soil boundary
⌐⌐⌐	Contour line
▬▬▬	Property line
210-A-0	Soil symbol
▭	Water

A.

B.

C.

D.

E.

F.

G.

H.

I.

Scale 1" = 100'

Plate 11. Gamewood Estates soil and topographical surveys. Interpretation-
project capability.

LEGEND

A. No temporary or continuing problems
B. Temporary problems, no continuing problems
C. Significant temporary problems, no continuing problems
D. Significant temporary problems, with continuing problems
E. Significant temporary problems, significant continuing problems
F. Significant temporary problems, complex continuing problems

G. Temporary & continuing complex problems, imposing extra design requirement
H. Temporary & continuing complex problems, imposing unusual design requirements
I. Temporary & continuing complex problems, imposing such design requirements that conventional urban uses are impractical

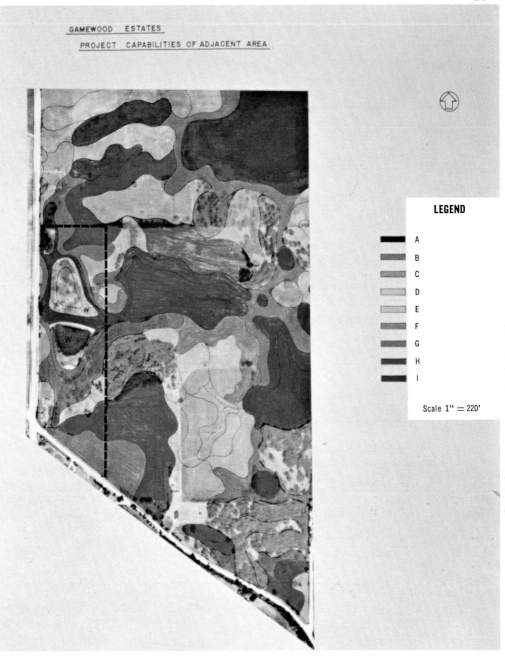

LEGEND

A
B
C
D
E
F
G
H
I

Scale 1″ = 220′

Plate 12. Gamewood Estates project capabilities of adjacent area.

LEGEND

A. No temporary or continuing problems
B. Temporary problems, no continuing problems
C. Significant temporary problems, no continuing problems
D. Significant temporary problems, with continuing problems
E. Significant temporary problems, significant continuing problems
F. Significant temporary problems, complex continuing problems

G. Temporary & continuing complex problems, imposing extra design requirement
H. Temporary & continuing complex problems, imposing unusual design requirements
I. Temporary & continuing complex problems, imposing such design requirements that conventional urban uses are impractical

SOIL LIMITATIONS FOR CAMP AREAS
(Intensive Use)

<u>NONE TO SLIGHT</u>

N — Well-drained, level and gently sloping soils

<u>MODERATE</u>

IM — Gravelly, gently sloping (2–8%) soils

2M — Sloping (8–15%) gravelly and shaly soils

<u>SEVERE</u>

IS — Very stony soils

2S — Wet soils

3S — Steep (15–25%) soils

Plate 13. Soil map shown in Chap. 10, Figure 1 (p. 111) interpreted to show limitations for intensive camping activities.

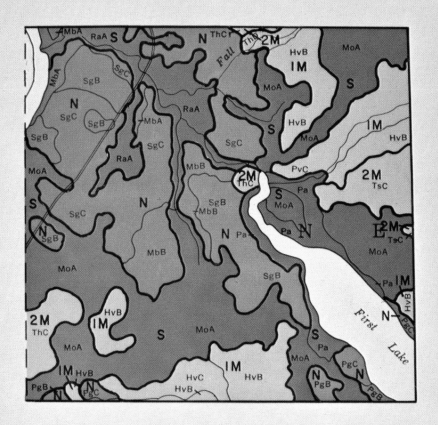

SOIL LIMITATIONS FOR PATHS AND TRAILS

NONE TO SLIGHT

| N | Well-drained, level to sloping soils |

MODERATE

| IM | Very stony sloping (2 - 15 %) soils |

| 2M | Sloping (8 - 25 %) shaly silty soils |

SEVERE

| S | Wet soils |

Plate 14. Soil map in Chap. 10, Figure 1 interpreted to show limitations for paths and trails.

SOIL LIMITATIONS FOR BUILDINGS IN RECREATIONAL AREAS

NONE TO SLIGHT

N Deep, well-drained, gently sloping (2 – 8 %) soils

MODERATE

M Sloping (8 – 15 %) soils

SEVERE

IS Very stony soils

2S Wet soils

2S Shallow sloping (8 – 25 %) soils

Plate 15. Soil map in Chap. 10, Figure 1 interpreted to show limitations for buildings in recreational areas.

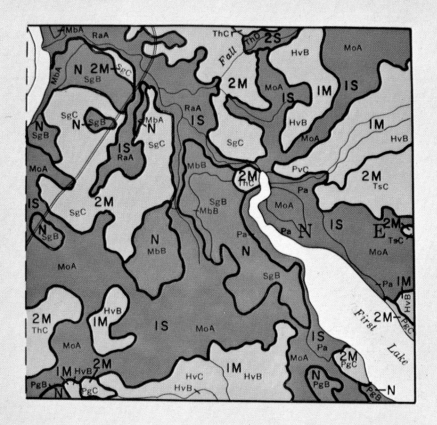

SOIL LIMITATIONS FOR PICNIC AREAS
(Intensive Use)

NONE TO SLIGHT

| N | Well-drained, level and gently sloping soils |

MODERATE

| IM | Very stony sloping (2 - 15 %) soils |

| 2M | Sloping (8 - 15 %) soils |

SEVERE

| IS | Wet soils |

| 2S | Steep (15 - 25 %) soils |

Plate 16. Soil map in Chap. 10, Figure 1 interpreted to show limitations for picnic areas subject to intensive use.

SOIL LIMITATIONS FOR PLAY AREAS
(Intensive Use)

NONE TO SLIGHT

| N | Level, well-drained soils |

MODERATE

| IM | Sloping (2 – 8 %) soils |

| 2M | Sloping (2 – 8 %) gravelly soils |

SEVERE

| IS | Very stony sloping (2 – 15 %) soils |

| 2S | Wet soils |

| 3S | Steeply sloping (8 – 25 %) soils |

Plate 17. Soil map in Chap. 10, Figure 1 interpreted to show limitations for intensive play areas.